The Straight Path

. . . .

A Religious Guide to
Finding and Fulfilling
One's Purpose

The Straight Path

· · · · · · ·

A Religious Guide to
Finding and Fulfilling
One's Purpose

CHRISTIAN EDWARD

TURNING
STONE
PRESS

Cover design by Frame 25 Productions
Interior design by Howie Severson

Turning Stone Press
8301 Broadway St., Ste. 219
San Antonio, TX 78209
www.turningstonepress.com

Library of Congress Control Number is
available upon request.

ISBN 978-1-61852-118-7

10 9 8 7 6 5 4 3 2 1

Printed in United States of America

*I am a servant of God, and I bring
a message of truth for the righteous.
Read it carefully, for it leads to
the straight path.*

The voice of one crying in the wilderness:
Prepare the way of the Lord,
make his paths straight.
Every valley shall be filled,
and every mountain and hill shall be brought low,
and the crooked shall be made straight,
and the rough ways shall be made smooth;
and all flesh shall see the salvation of God.

—Isaiah 40:3

As it is written in Isaiah the prophet,
"Behold, I send my messenger before thy face,
who shall prepare thy way:
the voice of one crying in the wilderness:
Prepare the way of the Lord, make his paths straight."

—Gospel of Mark 1:2

Such is the path of your Lord: a straight path.
We have made plain Our revelations to thinking men.
They shall dwell in peace with their Lord.
He will give them His protection as recompense for what they do.

—Quran 6:126–127

Arise! Watch. Walk on the right path. He who follows the right
path has joy in this world and in the world beyond.

—Buddha, Dhammapada 13:168

Humanity is the peaceful abode of men and righteousness is his straight path. What a pity for those who leave the peaceful abode and do not live there, and abandon the straight path and do not follow it!

—Mencius, book 4, part 1, chapter 10

Though this path is straight and narrow and sharp as the razor's edge, for me it has been the quickest and the easiest.

—Mahatma Gandhi, *My Experiments with Truth*

I have a dream that one day every valley shall be exalted, every hill and mountain shall be made low, the rough places will be made plain, and the crooked places will be made straight, and the glory of the Lord shall be revealed, and all flesh shall see it together.

—Dr. Martin Luther King Jr., "I Have a Dream"

Contents

Introduction

Each of us has a purpose. Sometimes we see it clearly. At other times, we lose sight of it. Hardship and suffering can cause us to doubt it. Yet even in our moments of greatest doubt and uncertainty, our purpose remains with us. It is an innate part of every human being. It drives us to better ourselves, to struggle, to create, and to evolve.

The steps we take to fulfil our purpose may differ. One person may devote their life to mastering the art of shaping wood and stone, another to raising a child, and another to freeing their people. Despite these different steps, though, the end is the same. It is to learn. It is to strengthen the mind and the body, and their connection to the soul, by acting virtuously and avoiding vice. It is to walk the straight path and draw closer to God.

The Bible, the Quran, and other sacred texts have explored the nature of the straight path. The Buddha, Mencius, Mahatma Gandhi, and other prophets and philosophers have devoted their lives to walking it. This guide draws upon what they have learned about the straight path and adds to their knowledge. It merges their wisdom with the insights we have gained about humanity's evolution through the study of evolutionary biology and epigenetics. This guide examines how thought and action shape evolution and how evolution is a physical, mental, and spiritual process of development. It explains how an individual's thoughts and actions shape their mind and body and how these mental and physical changes are passed to their children.

The Straight Path is organized into three Books. Book 1 focuses on the soul. It explains the nature of the straight path and how the straight path can be recognized and understood by observing God's signs, meeting and overcoming life's tests and challenges, and by reading what prophets and philosophers have learned about the straight path.

Book 2 focuses on the mind. It examines the nature of the mind and the mind's relationship to the soul and the body. It explains how the seven virtues strengthen and shape the growth of the mind and the body. It then examines how the seven vices weaken the mind and the body and retard their evolution.

Book 3 focuses on the body. It examines the nature of the body and the body's relationship to the soul and the mind. It describes how mental and physical discipline establish the proper relationship between the soul, the mind, and the body. It also explains how an individual can walk the straight path with others so as to benefit themselves and humanity as a whole.

The Straight Path provides guidance. It is a source of solace in times of need. It gives comfort when confronted by pain and suffering, and certainty when assailed by doubt and confusion. It strengthens faith in God when that faith wavers. And it gives direction to those who have lost their way.

You are never alone. The questions you ask yourself—such as "Is there more to life than just working and consuming?", "Why am I here?" and "What is my purpose?"—others ask, too. There are answers to those questions. The answers you seek lie along the straight path. Truth and justice lie along the straight path, as do happiness and freedom. And at the end of the straight path awaits God. This guide shall help you to find the straight path and walk it. It reveals a purpose that transcends the challenges of modern life.

The straight path is only ever a step ahead.

◞ Book 1 ◟

The Soul

I. The Soul

In the beginning, God took a part of Himself and shaped it into the eternal and divine soul. From the soul, He fashioned the mind; and from the mind, He molded the body. Each is connected to the other and responsible for the other.

To the soul, God gave authority over the mind; and to the mind, He gave authority over the body. This was the natural order set down by Him. It was just, for the soul is pure and the mind and the body are not.

And God said to the soul:

> "I give you this mind and body to learn of My creation. Only by strengthening them shall you learn about the universe and draw closer to Me."

From its creation, the soul desired to fulfil God's will by being truthful and just, for the soul knew that God cares for truth and justice above all things. God blesses the truthful and the just as they nourish His creation.

And God created many souls. And each soul sent its mind and body into the universe to learn of God's creation. And the minds and the bodies traveled far, and the souls learned much. But over time, some minds forgot their souls. They lost their way, for the universe was impure and held much distraction. They wandered blindly, beholden to their bodies. And the souls whose minds had lost their way cried out in anguish, for their minds could no longer hear them.

God watched and was dismayed by what these minds did. Yet He took pity on them, for they were ignorant. They were unaware of what they did to themselves and to God's creation. And in His pity, God gave these minds a gift to save them and guide them back to their souls. God showed them the straight path.

II. The Straight Path

The straight path is God's truth. It is the path of virtue and righteous action. It has always been and shall always be. It dwells in every grain of sand and on every mountain peak, in every mind, in every body, and in every soul.

The straight path is the purpose of the soul. It cleanses the soul's connection to the mind and enables the mind to hear the voice of the soul. It gives to the soul its proper authority over the mind and to the mind its proper authority over the body. It gives to the mind and the body the strength to act virtuously.

God laid the straight path to guide us to Heaven. And He gave us the freedom to choose to walk it or not. He gave us this choice to teach us the difference between right and wrong, so we remember the necessity for righteous action.

Those who walk the straight path shall walk it for their own good, and those who abandon the straight path shall abandon it at their own peril.

There are three steps to the straight path. The first step is to remember the straight path and begin to perceive its presence in all things. The second step is to seek the straight path by acting virtuously toward friends and enemies and rejecting vice. The third step is to find the straight path and, in spite of personal pain and suffering, act to strengthen humanity and fulfil the will of God.

The straight path passes many milestones and demands many deeds. It calls on some to raise children and others to resist corruption. Regardless of the deed, the straight path demands righteous action.

Those who walk the straight path cannot be distracted by greed when wealthy nor fear when poor. Nor can they be forced to bow to injustice, for they remain forever bound to their purpose, whether it leads them to fame or persecution.

God created the universe to test us and to teach us. Some shall go astray, while others shall walk the straight path. This is the choice God has laid in front of each of us. Woe to the corrupt who lead others away from the straight path. Woe to the corrupt who seek to make the straight path crooked. They reject God and choose instead to worship at the feet of their own vices. Pain and suffering shall be their lot. God shall leave the corrupt to suffer at the whims of the false gods of their own making.

Those who have faith in God shall walk the straight path, and God shall guide those who walk His straight path. The straight path gives the mind and the body the strength to act virtuously. It is the key to free from the chains of servitude those who are lost. It is the fulfilment of God's will in the universe, and it guarantees the survival of humanity.

God has provided the straight path for the righteous to bring justice to the Earth and to rectify humanity. Blessed are those who walk the straight path. Blessed are those who taste purpose and freedom.

III. Purpose

God gave to each soul a purpose. This purpose is to walk the straight path. Blessed are those who accept their purpose, for purpose endows the mind with strength. It feeds determination and acts as a support for the will when the will falters. It is a barrier against fear when fear tempts the mind to vice. It is the foundation of virtuous action.

When purpose is achieved, the length of a life becomes meaningless because the soul, the mind, and the body are fulfilled. Blessed are those who serve God and achieve their purpose.

Pity those who reject their purpose. They have lost their dream. They stumble forward in the dark, deaf to the entreaties of their soul. And because they cannot hear their soul, they lack an understanding of truth. Without an understanding of truth, of right and wrong, they are easily swayed by the wishes of others to act in a way that is harmful to themselves.

God demands more from us than just working and consuming. Money is not purpose. Work is not purpose. Consumption is not purpose. God created us to walk the straight path.

Woe to the corrupt who rob others of their purpose for their own selfish gain. Woe to the corrupt who obstruct others from fulfilling their purpose through enforced labor, worthless baubles, or lewd pursuits.

The corrupt weaken humanity and offend God, for they steal God's most precious gift: the straight path. God shall punish the corrupt. The corrupt shall be consumed by their own vices.

Yet those who have lost their purpose should not despair. They shall find it again, for the straight path is only ever a step ahead. Doubts and apathy may block the ears of the mind, but the soul is eternal and so is its purpose.

Your span has been allotted to you by God, so act with purpose. Avoid wasting time or the opportunities presented to you. Strengthen the mind and the body. This is God's will. We are here to serve the will of God.

Following the straight path appears a struggle to the ignorant. But to those who have begun to walk it, the straight path is the greatest of gifts.

IV. Freedom

God made each soul free. This is the soul's eternal condition. The mind and the body are free when they recognize and submit to the authority of the soul; and only when the mind and the body have achieved freedom can the soul fulfil its purpose.

The mind is free when it follows virtue and rejects vice. It is free when it listens to the soul and maintains its authority over the body. To do so, it must harden its will and discipline its thoughts and desires, so that it leads them rather than being led by them. Such a mind grows strong. It becomes an instrument of God's will. Blessed are those who control themselves so that they may help others.

The body is free when it follows the dictates of the mind. To do so, it must resist addiction and bad habits. The lungs must breathe air and the mouth must drink water and eat food, but the body can be free of those who wish to control or manipulate it. A body subservient to the mind is free.

Those who follow their every whim and desire are slaves. They are enslaved by their bodies, for they have made false gods of vice. Anger and self-loathing shall be their reward. A human is not a cow. One should never be dependent upon the whims of another, eating grass in a paddock, patiently waiting for the butcher to arrive. God demands more of us than this!

Freedom clears the ears, allowing the mind to hear the voice of the soul. Only when the mind and the body have achieved freedom can they discover their purpose and fulfil it. The free use their freedom to serve God and humanity. One cannot be free without walking the straight path.

V. Happiness

The happiness of worldly things—food, jobs, and holidays—is not true happiness. It is a passing shadow that cannot satisfy the soul. True happiness comes from fulfilling the purpose given to each of us by God. It comes from walking the straight path.

Satisfaction is not happiness. A cow is satisfied eating grass all day, but it has been bred to be satisfied. It has been conditioned before its birth to accept mental and physical weakness, to accept servitude. The soul of the cow screams in horror, but its mind cannot hear those screams, for the cow thinks only of the grass, the water, and the Sun. It is oblivious to what awaits it on the other side of the fence. God provides the cow as a lesson and a warning. Those who act like cows shall share the fate of cows.

Those who submit to the whims of the body become cows. They have lost happiness. The lazy are not happy nor are the greedy nor the lustful. They gain satisfaction from bodily delights, but these impulses are not happiness.

They are a brief respite in the darkness. They weaken the mind's control over the body and weaken the body itself. A body chained to desire is lethargic and lacks the strength to walk the straight path.

The body must learn self-discipline to achieve happiness. It must be strengthened. It must learn new skills and practice those skills so that it grows stronger. Only then can the body and the mind achieve freedom and walk the straight path. Only then are we happy.

VI. Signs

God created the universe and from His virtues fashioned laws to bind the universe. He created physical laws to control the movements of the stars, the orbits of the planets, and the rising and the falling of the seas. And He created moral laws so that the living grow, societies prosper, and humanity evolves. Without His physical laws, the planets and the stars would explode, and the seas would evaporate. Without His moral laws, the living would die and their societies would collapse: friend would turn against friend, the mother would slay her child, and the wolf would eat his cub.

Within God's laws lies the straight path. The straight path can be observed, but it cannot be changed nor molded to fit our desires.

God has placed signs in the universe to show us His straight path: a rainbow after a storm, a butterfly landing on a hand, a chance meeting with a friend, and the demise of the arrogant. He has also placed His signs in the books of the prophets: the Scriptures, the Gospels, the Quran, and other sacred texts. Read these books carefully, as they are books of instruction. God has placed His truth in these books for those who wish to find it.

Some argue that God's laws do not exist. Some argue that God's truth does not exist, that His truth is what each of us believes it to be. This error distracts the mind from the straight path.

God's signs are guides and warnings. Heed His warnings! Time and time again He has allowed the corrupt to destroy themselves. He shall do so in the future.

God did not place us on the Earth blind to right and wrong, blind to the truth, nor blind to the straight path. The straight path is clear to those who wish to see it. God's signs illuminate it.

Sometimes it appears that the innocent suffer as a result of God's signs. Have faith in God. He is beyond seeing and knowing, so do not presume to know the way events shall unfold. Sometimes a lesser pain is necessary to avoid a greater pain in the future. Have faith in God, for He shall rectify injustice at the most fortuitous moment.

Yet this is no excuse for inaction. Avoid sitting back, afraid, waiting for others to act. We are servants of God, and it is through us that justice is attained. Do what is right, walk the straight path, and become an instrument of God's will.

VII.   Tests

Life is suffering and life is joy. The mind and the body shall experience both and from this experience learn much, for God created the universe as their classroom, to test them and to teach them. God teaches us the lessons we need to learn. It is up to us to heed His lessons.

God's tests are gifts. They take many forms: success and failure, wealth and poverty, fame and persecution, loyalty and betrayal, birth and death. He tests the mind and the body in this way to strengthen them and prepare them for greater tests to come. The wise see a gift when the foolish are blind to it. Every hurt holds its lesson.

God demands that we learn and explore the universe. The sources of suffering are many, but nothing should deny the mind from learning and the body from acting while the body still lives. If you lose an arm, then you still have another arm. If you lose both arms, then you still have your toes and feet. If you lose all your limbs, then you still have your mouth. Only death is an excuse for inaction.

God tests the mind to strengthen its authority over the body. Avoid becoming addicted to pills and medicines. Avoid running to a doctor every time the body has a small ailment. The best cure for the body is sleep, exercise, and a healthy diet.

Trust your body. It has the ability to heal itself and overcome most diseases. Its resistance to disease has evolved in response to the diseases and ailments suffered by its ancestors. Your ancestors' efforts have strengthened your every cell. God rewards you for your ancestors' struggles. He who runs to the doctor every time he has an ailment loses self-control and becomes a slave to his body rather than master of it.

VIII. The Prophets

The prophets are God's messengers. Many of us cannot hear the voice of our souls nor see God's signs. So God sends His prophets to remind us of our purpose, to teach us of virtue and vice, and to guide us to the straight path. He sends His prophets to teach us that we are responsible for our own actions and that when we sin, we harm only ourselves. A child burns himself rather than his parent when he places his hand in a fire.

Pity those who refuse to learn from their mistakes. Pity those who close their ears and eyes to the truth. May they one day understand.

God is compassionate and patient. He waits for us to learn. And so He continues to send His prophets.

God has tailored each prophet's words to the ears of the listener. Through the prophets, He speaks of wheat to those who eat wheat and of rice to those who eat rice. His words may differ, but His message is the same. He speaks this way so that all may understand.

And how shall you know the prophet speaks the truth? You shall feel the truth of his words because his words shall resonate with all that you hold dear and good. They shall show you your soul.

Carefully read God's message in the words of the prophets. It shall strengthen and purify your mind by directing your thoughts toward virtue and away from vice. It shall direct you toward the straight path.

Close your ears to the words of false prophets. To those who claim right is wrong and wrong is right. To those who claim God's truth is a lie.

False prophets lie to confuse the innocent. They wish to deprive the innocent of purpose so as to enslave the innocent. They hate God, for His truth grants freedom. They are hypocrites! God has set the fate of the false prophet. Better it would be for the false prophet to cut out his tongue now than to utter another lie. For God reserves His greatest punishment for the corrupt who knowingly lead others from the straight path.

Have faith in yourself. Listen to your soul. Truth is there.

☙ Book 2 ❧

The Mind

I. The Mind

God created the mind as a bridge between the soul and
the body. The mind contains in equal portion the purity
of the first and the impurity of the second. This is necessary so that it can pass commands from one to the other.
In fashioning the mind, God also gave to it the will to
fulfil the soul's purpose and the desire to learn about the
Earth and the stars and the places in between. He also
gave to it the freedom to choose whether to listen to
the soul or to the body. This was necessary for the mind
to learn.

The brain produces thoughts in response to bodily
needs and genetic demands. It is the steering wheel, not
the driver. The mind is the driver. It decides the thoughts
to follow and the thoughts to ignore. It accepts some
thoughts and rejects others, and through this process,
shapes the brain to think in patterns. A strong mind listens to the soul and conditions the brain to produce virtuous thoughts. A weak mind grows beholden to bodily
desire and is forced by the brain to follow vice. Every
mind has the strength to choose.

God gave the mind this choice so that it would learn to establish its proper authority over the body. Woe to the mind that places the body above the soul and makes false gods of its own passions. Such a mind languishes in darkness, deaf to the cries of its soul. Blessed is the mind that places the soul over the body. Such a mind is a boon to humanity.

II.   Virtue

The seven virtues are love, compassion, humility, courage, honor, temperance, and piety. They come from God and infuse the soul. They are a part of the soul, its blood and bones.

The virtues guide righteous action, enabling the righteous to implement God's will in the universe. Those blessed with virtue possess all they need. They never grow weary. Nor do they hunger or thirst.

Thought and action shape the mind and the body. Just as strong muscles make a body strong, so virtue makes the mind strong. Virtue enables the mind to think more clearly. It relieves the mind of indecision and grants the mind certainty in its actions. It makes the mind more responsive to the commands of the soul and the body more responsive to the commands of the mind.

Only by following the demands of the soul and acting virtuously can we be certain of fulfilling God's will. Only those who act virtuously walk the straight path.

Love

Love is the breath of God. It is to be bound to another and from this binding to experience joy. It is to give rather than take, to serve rather than be served, and to act for the benefit of others so they may grow strong.

Love binds man to woman and woman to man, parent to child and child to parent, friend to friend, family to society, society to family, and all to God. It is the virtue that binds all relationships together. Without love there would be no family, no society, and no humanity.

Love is a part of all virtue and the foundation of all virtue. From love come compassion, humility, courage, honor, temperance, and piety. And from love flow respect, trust, and self-sacrifice. He who loves walks the straight path.

Love is God's whiteboard, His teaching tool. By loving others, we learn more about them. And by loving others, we also learn more about ourselves. The more we love, the more we learn. God wants us to learn and grow strong. Blessed are God's lessons.

Love is to be bound to God. All things are a part of God and all share in His love. The straight path is a sign of God's love. The farther we walk along the straight path, the closer we come to God. And the closer we come to God, the more we comprehend the beauty of His creation. God laid the straight path for us so that we can achieve salvation.

God is the source of love. Love radiates from God into the soul. From the soul, it flows into the mind; and from the mind, it fills the body. It opens the mind to the commands of the soul, and in turn fortifies the body. The love that flows from the soul is a torrent that washes away all fear.

Do not confuse love with vice. Love is not jealousy. It is not control. It is not fear. And it is not lust. Love strengthens the mind and the body. It does not weaken them.

To lose love is to lose the soul. The mind without love becomes a wasteland, prey to apathy, hatred, and fear. Deaf to its soul, it loses hope and purpose. It stumbles forward, searching beyond the horizon for what lies at its feet. It loses sight of the beauty surrounding it, of the beauty in other people, and of the beauty in itself. It loses the will to continue. Pity those who lose love. May God help them to find it again and to walk the straight path.

Love is to be bound to a husband or a wife. Blessed is the love a husband and a wife hold for each other. Each challenge shared, encouraging word, and supportive glance tightens the bond between them. And as the bond between them tightens, the more strength each of them draws from this bond. Blessed are the lovers. They are God's builders.

Pity the husband who harms his wife by word or deed or leaves her for greed, fame, or lust. He betrays his wife. Pity the wife who harms her husband by word or deed or leaves him for greed, fame, or lust. She betrays her husband. They also betray themselves, for to betray another is to submit to vice and step from the straight path.

God created man and woman to complement each other's strengths and in so doing strengthen humanity. He created man and woman to form a family and from the union of husband and wife to create children. A family grows strong when the love between husband and wife is strong. A strong family strengthens a society, and a strong society strengthens humanity, for the family is the basis of society and society is the basis of humanity. Blessed is the family, the guardian of humanity's survival.

God created the family to love and nurture children. The love parents feel for their children is an endless spring. Never does it run dry, even in the scorching heat of anger, for this love comes from the soul, pure and unsullied. God placed the strong in the world to protect the weak. May we fulfil our duty to our children to protect and strengthen them. We survive in them. Children are the beginning and the end. Children are the seeds of humanity.

Love is God's messenger. It tells parents of their duty: to nourish the gift God has given to their children. This gift is the straight path. Children are born knowing the straight path. They are born knowing truth, justice, and love. Only the distractions of the physical world can make them forget these things.

Parents strengthen their children by teaching their knowledge and skills to their children. A skill is more precious than any toy, for once a child has learned a skill, he is strengthened by that skill. The child who knows how to fish can catch his own fish. He no longer needs to wait for someone else to feed him, for he can feed himself. He has learned how to survive. Blessed are the parents who teach their children how to feed themselves. They have freed their children. Blessed are those who free others. They strengthen humanity.

How a lesson is taught is as important as what a lesson teaches. Parents must teach their children with respect and love. Respect and love inspire trust. Once children trust their parents, they can learn the most difficult lesson because they know it is for their benefit.

Children soak up knowledge as a sponge soaks up water. They are born with the need to discover new things and explore the universe, just as they are born with the need to breathe, eat, drink, and love. God gave them this need to encourage them to learn and strengthen themselves. Woe to those who stifle a child's need to learn. They obstruct the will of God.

Great is the duty of parents to set the right example for their children: to walk straight and to act virtuously so that their children learn the difference between right and wrong. Blessed are the parents who guide their children to virtue and away from vice. Who instill in their children courage and show their children how to conquer fear. Who guide their children to their souls and give to their children the strength to achieve their purpose. Such children shall be boons to humanity.

Woe to the parents who refuse to fulfil their duty to love and strengthen their children because of greed, fame, or lust. They betray and weaken their children. They confuse the significant with the insignificant. They lack wisdom. Every act has its consequence. Their vices shall consume them.

Pity the parents who must leave their children in the care of others; who must trust others to teach their children the difference between right and wrong. Profound is their anguish, but they should not despair. God is always watching over their children and their children's teachers.

Great is the responsibility of teachers in shaping the thoughts and actions of the children in their care. Just as a piece of cotton dyed in indigo colors another piece of cotton it touches, so do the thoughts and actions of one mind color the thoughts and actions of another mind. The wise teacher teaches the child history, science, languages, and mathematics. He teaches the child about virtue and vice and the straight path. He sets an example for the child to follow. Having walked farther along the straight path, he shows the child the direction of the straight path and how to walk it. He teaches the child that the child can walk the straight path. The wise teacher labors for God.

Love is to be bound to a parent. Children love their parents when they fulfil their duty to their parents. Their duty is to cherish, respect, and learn from their parents. Parents are wise. They have learned much from their experiences and wish to teach what they have learned to their children so that their children avoid the same mistakes they have made. The wise child heeds his parents' advice and is strengthened by it. The ignorant child turns his back on wisdom.

Children should treat their parents with dignity and respect. They should speak kind words to their parents and show them no sign of impatience. They should feed and clothe their parents when their parents can no longer feed and clothe themselves; their parents loved and nurtured them when they were young and helpless. Children should do the same for their parents when their parents are old and helpless. Every kindness demands a kindness in return.

Love is to be bound to a friend. Great is the gift of friendship, a gift that cannot be bought. Choose loyal and honest friends who strengthen rather than weaken you. They shall help you in times of struggle. When others reject you, they shall accept you; when others lie to you, they shall speak the truth to you; and when others betray you, they shall protect you.

Blessed is he who aids his friend in his labors so that his friend has four hands instead of two, who helps his friend to build his house in six months instead of a year. It pleases God that we struggle together. God helps those who help each other.

Avoid false friends who care only for themselves. Avoid the flatterer, the capricious, or the jealous. They shall harm and betray you. Pity those who cannot tell a false friend from a true friend. Their souls warn them. They just need to listen.

Love is to be bound to a society. Blessed is the society that loves its people. A society that loves its people strengthens its people. Its leaders pass laws for the benefit of all and not just the few. It lifts the weak who fall, through no fault of their own, so that all may prosper. Such a society is led by the righteous.

Pity the society that hates its people. A society that hates its people weakens its people. Its leaders pass laws for the benefit of the few and to the detriment of the many. They care only for their own privilege and ease, heedless of the harm they cause to their people.

Such leaders are distracted by arrogance and greed. Better the people remove them now than join them in the abyss; for vice rots all things, and a society led by the corrupt is destined to fall.

A society chooses its path and is responsible for its actions. God leaves corrupt societies on Earth as a lesson to humanity, so that humanity can learn the difference between right and wrong and the consequences of virtue and vice. God does this so that humanity can survive. The rotten limb falls so that the tree may live.

Compassion

Compassion is to feel pity for those who suffer and to act to ease their suffering. It is to know all are equal and deserve to be treated with dignity and respect. Treat others as you want them to treat you. This is the essence of compassion and the basis of the straight path.

God created all souls, minds, and bodies equal. All share kinship with God and shall return to God. So let compassion guide your actions. Treat others with the respect and dignity they deserve as one of God's creations.

Even the corrupt deserve to be treated with compassion. God loves the corrupt despite their wrongdoings, for the corrupt are lost. They are deaf to their souls and are blind to right and wrong. They know not what they do.

Forgive the corrupt and resist their wrongdoings. Help them see their mistakes so that they may walk the straight path again, strengthen themselves, and strengthen humanity. Blessed are the repentant who turn back to God. God waits to embrace them.

Compassion compels the mind to act justly and to resist the enslavement of others through fear, addiction, or enforced labor. Enslavement arises from arrogance. It arises from the delusion that one person is better than another and deserves more than another. This delusion weakens a society because it destroys the bonds of trust and respect that bind people together. Compassion strengthens the ties binding a society together and helps a society to prosper. Without compassion, humanity shall perish.

All minds feel compassion. Compassion is a natural part of the mind, just as the eyes are a natural part of the body. Without thinking, a passerby shall rush to the aid of a baby who falls into a river. He acts not for his own benefit, to gain the praise of others or to receive some reward, but because he knows it is the right thing to do. His soul tells him this.

Yet beware. As the eyes can be destroyed, so can compassion. Fear destroys compassion. Pity those who refuse to act through fear; who allow fear to overwhelm their compassion and grow indifferent to the suffering of others. Pity those who turn their eyes away from the man being beaten or close their ears to the screams of the woman being raped. Pity those who allow others to be excluded from society because of difference. They hurt themselves when they refuse to help those in pain. They allow fear to conquer their minds, and by doing so, relinquish the authority of their minds to their bodies. Heavy indeed is the burden of guilt they carry. May they see the burden and free themselves of it.

Compassion is a warning: a warning against stepping from the straight path. It protects the mind against guilt. It protects the mind against the lies and propaganda of the corrupt who try to inspire hatred and greed in others so as to exploit them.

It is right to help the sick and the poor. Those who suffer pain and hardship are God's witnesses on Earth. Blessed are those who share their water with the thirsty in the desert. Their water shall be replenished tenfold. Blessed are those who give their change to the beggar on the street. Their wealth shall be replenished tenfold. Blessed are those who sacrifice themselves for humanity. They draw closest to God.

Humility

Wisdom is the proper weighing of things. Humility is wisdom, for the humble properly weigh their strengths and weaknesses and, from this weighing, see the purpose God has given to them and seek to fulfil it. Humility is to serve the will of God.

Humility is to serve others before oneself. The humble farmer grows food to feed others because that is the farmer's strength. The humble teacher teaches others how to learn because that is the teacher's strength. The humble prophet speaks God's message because that is the prophet's strength. Thus, each in their own way benefits humanity and walks the straight path.

The humble refuse to boast of their good deeds. They lack the need to attract the praise of others, for the deed is reward enough. They are neither self-righteous nor arrogant. They know all are equal and they refuse to place themselves above others. Even a child can teach a prophet.

The humble treat others with respect and dignity. They look at others with open eyes and an open face, never down their nose or in a haughty way. They devote their time to others and avoid rushing out of impatience. They speak to others in a pleasant and firm tone, never battering others with their words as the arrogant do who presume their words are more important than those of others. They avoid judgment. By acting humbly toward others, we act humbly toward God.

Humility comes with greater understanding. As the mind learns more, it gains a better understanding of itself and the purpose God has given to it. It learns the proper weighing of things. This is wisdom. It neither overestimates nor underestimates itself. And from this understanding, it conquers arrogance and fear and strengthens its authority over the body. We are stars in an infinite universe.

The humble know their strengths and use them properly to better themselves and others. But they avoid reveling in their strengths. To revel in one's strengths is to grow infatuated by them and fall prey to the delusions of arrogance and pride. The arrogant waste their strengths and lose them. Pity those who waste God's gifts.

The humble accept their strengths and so retain their self-respect and dignity. The mind that loses dignity grows fearful. It doubts itself and no longer believes it is worthy of God's gifts nor good enough to fulfil God's will. How comforting excuses are to the fearful. What delusion. God made all minds equal and worthy instruments of His will. Blessed are the humble who use their strengths to lead others to the straight path.

The humble see their defects and accept them. They give a task to another if they are more capable to complete it so that all may benefit. And because the humble see their defects, they are able to rectify them. A thing unseen cannot be fixed.

The humble kneel before God and willingly submit themselves to God. They accept the span God has allotted to them and the role God has fashioned for them. Humility enables the mind to loosen its grip of the ego, to put aside its selfish aims and instead devote itself to fulfilling God's will. The humble mind is an instrument of God.

Be humble before the future and plan vigilantly for each possible outcome, but avoid preempting events. To preempt an event, to simply hope that the future shall transpire as desired, is arrogance and folly. Even the prescient cannot shape events. Only God can do this. Only God knows what He has allotted to each of us.

The humble understand this and face the future with patience and calm. They accept the future and the course of God's plan. They act when it is time to act, never too early nor too late. To act at the proper moment is to pick the grape at its sweetest. God rewards the patient.

Courage

Courage is the fire of God. It is to meet fear and overcome fear. It is to struggle against injustice and resist oppression.

It is to act righteously in spite of personal suffering. It is to fulfil the will of God and walk the straight path.

Courage inspires us to seek out new places and discover new things. It inspires us to learn and strengthen our minds and bodies. This is God's will. God commands us to learn and strengthen ourselves, for only by doing so shall humanity survive.

Woe to those who refuse to learn and strengthen themselves. Woe to those who wallow in sloth and fear and accept the weakening of their minds and bodies. They sin against themselves. Their time is limited.

Courage rids the mind of docility and enables the mind to overcome fear. It calms the mind and allows the body to act at the opportune moment. It breeds confidence and inspires courage in others. By acting courageously we become wolves instead of cows, ever ready to maul the hand of the butcher.

The fearful refuse to act. And because they refuse to act they lose the ability to act. They lose the ability to uphold right and resist wrong. They become docile. Fear weakens the mind and the body. Pity those who allow their wrists to be shackled.

Courage has ever bested fear, for courage comes from the soul while fear comes from the body. Courage is remembered, not taught. Every mouth can refuse to lie. Every mind can control fear. Take heart and have confidence in yourself. Draw on the courage that lies within you. All God wants of any of us is that we do the best we can with what He has given to us. He has made all of us capable of walking the straight path.

Courage is the harbinger of God's justice. It compels us to struggle against injustice alone when others refuse. It compels the mouth to say "no" when others say "yes" and the body to remain standing when others kneel. It compels the mind to receive the world's pain and return it with love. Blessed is he who preserves the truth against a shower of lies. The most courageous suffer alone for the benefit of all.

To struggle is to strive toward a goal despite suffering. God has given to each of us the strength to struggle and the courage to act righteously. He commands us to seek justice and struggle against injustice, to obey just laws and struggle against unjust laws, to defend just systems and struggle against unjust systems. Injustice is corruption, and God demands that we struggle against corruption so that humanity may prosper.

Know when to resist and know when to yield. Step forward when justice can be attained through resistance. Step back when justice can be attained through yielding.

Know when to resist using nonviolence and violence. Resist nonviolently when the wrongdoer listens to his conscience or is reliant upon those he abuses for the accumulation of his authority and wealth. Either his own conscience or the fear of losing his privileges shall force him to desist. Sanity cannot exist without a conscience. A leech cannot feed without a body.

Blessed is he who turns the other cheek, who receives the blows of the wrongdoer with silence and a steady gaze without trembling or speaking angry words in return. Such courage gains the respect of the wrongdoer and forces him to listen to his conscience, understand the wrong he has committed, and step back onto the straight path.

Blessed is he who writes, speaks, or marches to make others aware of injustice and who harnesses the strength of others to overcome injustice. Blessed is he who refuses to labor for the wrongdoer, use the wrongdoer's services, or consume the wrongdoer's products, who forces the wrongdoer to realize that he did not create but rather stole his wealth. The wealth of the slave owner is not his own, for he did not earn it with his own hands.

Resist violently when the wrongdoer is insane and revels in the harm he causes to others. When the wrongdoer is deaf to his conscience and refuses to listen to his soul, then it is right to defend oneself with fist and teeth. It is right to block the claw that threatens the eye. This is God's will. Blessed is he who defends himself against the abuse of others. Blessed is he who defends others with his own words and body and protects those who cannot protect themselves. God molded the hands and the feet to protect the body and to protect other bodies.

God commands us to defend the weak and the helpless, the old men, old women, and children against a wrongdoer, whether that wrongdoer be a person, a corporation, or a nation. The strong must protect the weak. This is the duty God has given to those who walk the straight path.

Never permit the corrupt to abuse the innocent. To do so is to condone sin and be tainted by sin. It is to step from the straight path. This is a little death worse than death itself. Better to die resisting than to accept genocide: better Warsaw than Auschwitz. Strive for a noble death.

Fulfilling the purpose of the soul is more important than the length of a life. By walking the straight path, we free others from servitude and strengthen humanity. Great indeed are Jesus Christ, Joan of Arc, Mahatma Gandhi, and Dr. Martin Luther King Jr. Each sacrificed their life to free humanity. Each walked the straight path. At the end, there is only one question to answer: "How well did I serve others?"

God forbids the killing of the innocent. Not even the smallest act of evil is justified to achieve the greater good, for evil creates only evil. Only the just act pleases God. Act righteously, even when you fear it will cause pain or you might fail. Have faith in God. He shall help you. God protects the righteous and the seekers of truth.

Beware of acting the hypocrite. Beware of treating the corrupt as they would treat you, dressing evil acts in self-righteous robes. Compassion is the foundation of all righteous action. It is the foundation of God's justice. All deserve to be treated with dignity, not just in action but in thought as well. Even the corrupt who have been led astray by their vices deserve to be forgiven, because their soul, like yours, comes from God. And one day they shall hear their soul and fulfil God's will.

Follow your conscience. It is the voice of your soul, an echo of God's will. It can see truth just as the eye can see a path. Those who refuse to listen to their conscience refuse to listen to their soul. Beware, if you stop listening to the soul, it shall stop speaking.

Pity those who have lost contact with their soul. They have ripped the vine from the earth and destroyed the fruit. Without the soul, the mind and the body shall wither.

God shows us through our conscience that only virtuous action strengthens the mind and the body. He shows us that we can achieve happiness only if we follow our conscience. Time and time again, He has shown us how we suffer if we reject it. And He shall show us again in the future. God is patient. Our conscience shows us our soul. Our conscience shows us God.

Honor

Honor is to act with respect and dignity toward oneself and others. It is to think the truth, speak the truth, and act truthfully. It is achieved when thought, word, and act are one.

Honor is to respect one's own thoughts and actions. It is to like oneself and maintain one's dignity, for dignity is self-honor. This is achieved by walking the straight path. Those who maintain their dignity, who hold on to their inner sense of truth and faith in God, cannot be conquered. Their bodies may be crushed, but their minds shall grow strong.

Honor cleanses the mind of guilt. It restores the mind's sense of self-worth and reminds the mind of its own innate goodness. It strengthens the mind's control over the body and enables the mind to identify and reject arrogance, prejudice, cowardice, and fear. Such vices cannot take root in an honorable mind.

Honor is a mountain stream free of impurity. No mud clouds the honorable act. Its motivation is clear. The honorable do what they say they shall do and can be depended upon to keep their word. They are reliable. They do not need to sign contracts because they honor truth and are bound by it. They understand that to lie is to lose truth and to lose truth is to step from the straight path. Their word binds them more strongly than a piece of paper ever could.

Honor is to conduct commerce fairly. Treat others as you would be treated and sell them things that you would buy. You are responsible for what you sell, so sell only food that you would eat, water that you would drink, and clothes that you would wear. Sell only objects of the best quality that fulfil their role properly. Then you shall strengthen those who buy from you.

Never sell a thing simply to make a profit, to feed an addiction, or to create one. Never sell a thing to weaken another. Those who enslave others for profit have fallen to greed. They have turned away from God and have chosen to kneel at the feet of Mammon. One cannot serve two masters. Those who cannot be trusted with the riches of the Earth cannot be trusted with the riches of Heaven. The greedy cannot walk the straight path.

Honor is to be loyal to others. It is to help and protect others. Never betray another, for to betray another is to hurt another and to act against the will of God. To betray another is to step from the straight path.

All people are equal and all people deserve to be treated equally with respect and dignity. Always promote dignity in others and an understanding of their own self-worth. Strengthen the dignity of others by treating them with respect. By treating others with respect, you also strengthen your own dignity. Strong indeed is the dignified mind assured of its purpose. It carries a shield of truth that no lie can penetrate.

Honor strengthens all relationships. It binds a family firmly together. Act honorably toward your parents and children, and they shall act honorably toward you. When all members of a family honor one another, then they shall trust one another and help one another to learn and grow strong. All shall prosper.

By strengthening a family, honor also strengthens a society. When a family grows strong, so does the society of which it is a part. Honor also strengthens humanity. When a society grows strong, so does humanity, of which it is a part. Blessed are the honorable, for their acts strengthen all.

Treat friends and enemies with honor. Praise righteous acts and oppose wrongful acts, but avoid abusing or treating unjustly those who commit wrongful acts. The human and the act are separate. There are wrongful acts, but the mind that commits such acts is mistaken, not evil. It is deaf to its soul and lacks guidance and, as a consequence, falls prey to ignorance, hatred, and fear.

Beware the comforts of arrogance and resist judging others. There are no perfect minds. All minds experience fear and confusion. And all minds make mistakes. God made the mind this way so that it learns.

Treat those who commit wrongful acts with respect and dignity. Help them learn from their mistakes and lead them back to the straight path. Many a traveler has taken the wrong road through no fault of their own.

God gave the body hands and feet, eyes and ears so that the body can strengthen itself and the mind can learn about the universe. To give up is to stay ignorant; to struggle is to learn. There is an honorable way to struggle. This is to resist injustice with dignity. If everyone took an eye for an eye, then the world would be blind; but if no one resisted their eye being taken, then the world would also be blind. God wants you to see. He placed you here to serve.

Honor is to fulfil the will of God and to walk the straight path. It is to live the life God has given, not to avoid death nor to run to death so as to escape God's will. To do so is both cowardly and dishonorable.

There are many ways to lose dignity. Never perform lewd acts or sell the body for money. These weaken the mind. A mind stripped of its dignity lacks the strength to walk the straight path.

Never strip another of their dignity. To make a human not human is evil. Never lie to another to gain advantage over them. Liars lack respect for themselves and for those to whom they lie. Lies and corruption rob the mind of dignity.

Avoid lust and greed. Vice drains dignity and weakens the mind. It pulls the mind from the straight path. The mind must control the body. There is no worse a fate for the mind than to become a slave to the body's every whim. Such a body becomes a prison for the mind. Act with honor, foster dignity, and you shall have the strength to act righteously.

The greatest honor is to serve God. Act honorably and you shall perceive your purpose more clearly and step onto the straight path more quickly.

Temperance

Temperance is to restrain and moderate bodily desire. It is to discipline the body and strengthen the mind. It is to give the mind its proper place and to allow the mind and the body to fulfil their purpose. Each act of restraint is a further step along the straight path.

Temperance instils in the body a thirst for righteousness. It makes the body a servant of the mind. The temperate mind wields the body with as little effort as the farmer does the scythe, ever ready to reap God's harvest.

Without temperance, the mind cannot control the body. A body uncontrolled by the mind becomes a slave to vice. It grows weak and lethargic, neither willing to listen to the commands of the mind nor able to heed the will of God. Such a body cannot walk the straight path.

Live a temperate life. Restrain corrupt and bitter thoughts. Ignore ideas of lust, greed, fear, and hate. Do this and virtuous action shall follow. Action follows thought.

Only a body cleansed of vice can serve the mind. Only a body cleansed of vice can hear the voice of the soul.

God measures each life. He fills each vessel to the brim. And with each passing moment a drop is lost, never to be replaced and never to return. So use the life God has given to you. It is a gift with a purpose. Avoid wasting time. Avoid superfluous acts that weaken the mind and the body. Avoid watching television and playing games that teach nothing. Avoid falling prey to sloth. Gather the moments and use them to strengthen the mind and the body, to learn more and serve others better. Use the moment to step onto the straight path.

Temperance strengthens the body. Only eat and drink natural fruits and vegetables, grains, and meat, for these clear the brain and make the body strong and nimble. Eat and drink enough to keep the body healthy, not too much nor too little. In this way, the body shall be free of gluttony and sloth. It shall avoid becoming a slave to taste. Avoid processed foods filled with salt and sugar. These are addictive. Avoid genetically modified foods. These have been created for profit, not human health. They are poison and weaken the body. A body that consumes these things cannot fulfil the demands of the mind and the soul.

If the source of your food and drink is untrustworthy, then grow your own. If a parcel of earth can be found, then use it to grow fruit, vegetables, grains, and meat and to collect water. Treat the earth with respect and return to it what you take. Learn the seasons and the weather, and the harvest shall be bountiful. Pity he who has forgotten how to grow his own food. He is a baby dependent on others to feed him.

Avoid drugs and stimulants. Drugs give pleasure, not happiness. Stimulants ease tiredness for a time, but they quickly take back what they have given and more. Both are addictive. Addiction weakens the body. The body enslaved by addiction is unwilling to listen to the commands of the mind and the soul. It heeds only the cries of its addiction. Addiction is evil because it robs the body of its purpose.

Refrain from buying and consuming things simply for pleasure. These things cannot help you achieve your purpose and attain happiness. Yearn for what you need, not for what you want. Keep your possessions few. The more you have, the more you carry. And the more you carry, the more the things you carry shall distract you from the straight path.

Wear well-fashioned clothes that keep the body warm and dry in winter and cool in summer. Wear clothes that last for many years, not just a few months. Use well-made tools that are strong, reliable, and do not break. Create a thing to last a lifetime. This conserves the Earth's resources: wood, minerals, water, and air. Those who eat all their wheat in the summer have none for the winter. They are wasteful so they suffer, and if they don't learn then they die. This is God's law.

Keep your surroundings simple and functional and your home adequate to your needs: a room with a bed, a desk to write on, a shelf for books, and a living space to meet friends. One human does not need ten rooms. Foster simplicity and beauty, as God loves these things. God loves the symmetry of a leaf and the color of a flower. Beauty gladdens the soul, for beauty comes from God.

God created the Earth as a haven for humanity. The Earth shelters us against the cold and allows us to live.

But it is not eternal. It has a life as we do. Its minerals, its water, and its air are limited. Yet the greedy act as if they are not. They take without returning and care only for today, heedless of next year. They dismiss the lives of those to come.

God sends the floods, the storms, and the droughts as warnings, but the greedy refuse to heed His signs. Humanity can survive only through temperance, by saving what it has, making things better, and reusing what it can. All must do this, not just a few. Each is connected to the other and responsible for the other. We prosper from temperance and suffer from greed.

Create what is needed. Never overproduce to simply make a profit. Profit tempts the greedy to exploit and enslave others. Overproduction wastes resources and wastes time—time that the mind and the body should use to learn more and strengthen themselves.

It is right to stop the greedy child from eating the food of other children. If this is not done, then the other children starve. Resist the greedy who prefer to let others starve than to lose their own delicacies. God sends the righteous to resist the greedy. Live a temperate life and survive. This is the straight path.

Piety

Piety is to love God and honor God. It is to submit to God, serve God, and act according to the will of God.

Piety arises from action rather than intention. It is to act virtuously, to help rather than hinder, to raise up rather than pull down, and to love rather than hate. It is to fulfil the will of God.

Piety is to respect God and thank Him for what He has given to us. It is to show this thanks through prayer.

Prayer pleases God because it draws us closer to Him. It strengthens our bond with God and opens our ears to His voice. It leads us to truth.

Pray to God and ask for His guidance. He shall answer you if you listen. Be honest with Him as you would with yourself, for He comprehends your intention even if you do not. He sees all and knows all. He is your eyes and your ears, your toes and your fingers. He is the air that blows your hair and the rain that pelts your cheek. He is closer to you than your skin. He is witness to your every thought and deed, to your every word, spoken or not, good or bad.

Nothing can be hidden from God—in the past, the present, or the future. It is to your benefit, not His, that you speak the truth to Him. For the greater the truth you speak to God, the more you shall understand His straight path.

Kneel before God and strip yourself of all conceit. Tell Him only the truth, and the truth shall strengthen your bond with Him. Ask Him to help you walk the straight path, and He shall answer your prayer. Ask and you shall receive.

Prayer gives solace in times of need. It strengthens faith in God and the feeling of His presence: a feeling of warmth, the knowledge of right, that radiates throughout the mind and the body.

Hold fast to your faith in God when others laugh at you and jeer. Do not be afraid. You are never alone. God is always close. He is never more than the width of a hair away. He is standing beside you in the dark, waiting to pick you up when you falter and guide you back to Him. God protects his servants.

Have faith in God, and He shall give you the strength you need to act righteously. He shall give you the strength to complete your purpose and walk the straight path.

God reminds the pious of His presence every day in the smallest and greatest of things—in a change in the wind and the rising of the Sun.

Pity those who have lost faith in God. They doubt God's presence because they no longer hear the voice of their soul.

Pity those who refuse to listen to their souls. They harm themselves. Without faith they are lost. They drift becalmed upon a sea of humanity.

Pity those who refuse to believe; they are consumed by doubt. Doubt is ever the greedy master. He has driven many into the darkness and waylaid many more. Yet he is weak, for he is fear's child. He can only pester the mind beholden to the body. He dares not confront the mind subject to the soul, for faith comes from the soul, and faith has ever bested doubt.

Great indeed is the faith that comes from earnest prayer. It is a spring that quenches the driest throat. It is right to pray during times of need, when the will falters and belief in God is tested. But prayer is no excuse for inaction. It is no excuse for laziness or for inadequate preparation. It is no excuse for not acting to the best of one's ability in any task that arises; for it is through discipline and self-control that God's benefits flow.

God loves the prayers of the pious. Yet more than prayer, God loves the virtuous act. For the virtuous act achieves God's will. Prayer is simply the intention, whereas the virtuous act is the intention fulfilled. Better to act virtuously than to pray. One virtuous act shall set your feet on the straight path more quickly than a hundred prayers ever could.

III. Vice

The seven vices are hatred, envy, arrogance, cowardice, lust, greed, and sloth. They breed in a body infatuated by the distractions of the physical world, in a body which has rebelled against the authority of the mind.

Vice weakens the body. It compels the body to steal, to cheat, to slander, to betray, and to perform lewd acts. It drains the body's life. It wastes the muscles and withers the bones. Witness the corrupt man, his hair grey and his body filled with disease of thought and flesh. The body enslaved by vice shall die before its time.

Vice weakens the mind. It forces the mind to turn its attention away from the soul and to the body. It compels the mind to kneel at the feet of the body's cravings and addictions. Such a mind grows deaf to the commands of the soul. It forgets the soul and becomes confused. It no longer understands virtue. Having lost its understanding of right and wrong, it steps from the straight path. Pity the mind whose body has become its prison.

Yet vice can only distract the mind, not conquer it. The mind knows it harms itself when it follows vice. It feels guilt for its wrongful deeds. Only the truly insane, those whose minds are damaged, feel nothing when they hurt others or themselves. Guilt is a message from the soul, a message to the mind that even vice cannot shout down.

The mind feels guilt because it knows that each wrongful act it commits takes it farther from the straight path, farther away from achieving its purpose and the purpose of its soul. It senses, however vaguely, that it can only find the straight path by virtuous deeds, but its body denies it this.

The mind knows it weakens itself each time it succumbs to vice. It learns that each wrongful act it commits further undermines its authority over the body. It feels vice gnawing at its confidence and dignity. It senses its determination being extinguished and its ability to take control of the body and fashion it into an instrument of God's will being lost. Smothered by vice, the mind grows to hate itself and its body. He who sins, sins against himself.

The mind is both judge and jury of its own actions. It is hostage to its own deeds. It cannot ignore guilt. It must accept guilt if it wishes to be free of guilt. Only through virtuous action can the mind forgive itself for the wrong it has committed. And only through virtuous action can it regain authority over the body. Only virtue washes the stain from the cloth. The righteous carry no burdens.

Hatred

Hatred is to desire to harm another and to act upon that desire. It is to ignore the conscience. It is to ignore the voice of the soul.

Hatred harms the body and the mind. It denies the body rest. It tightens the stomach and grinds the teeth. It drains the body's energy to feed itself and wastes the body's vitality until the body withers and grows decrepit.

The mind dominated by hate is enslaved. It is chained to its hatred and compelled to focus upon the object of its hate: to always taste it, smell it, hear it, and see it.

Hatred perverts the mind's perception. It compels the mind to see only what it wants the mind to see. It compels the mind to see only the wrong in another and never the right. It compels the mind to believe that all are evil, all are responsible, all are worthless, and all deserve vengeance. This is delusion. Nationality, race, ideology, and religion do not make a human evil.

Hatred stops the mind from learning. The mind that hates a thing refuses to learn about that thing. It refuses to understand the reasons for that thing's success or failure. It denies itself valuable lessons. Pity the mind that refuses to learn and strengthen itself.

Hatred makes the mind vulnerable to the manipulations of the corrupt who inflame the mind's anger for their own selfish gain. It pushes the mind toward greater vice. It draws the mind away from the soul and makes the mind subject to the body.

Hatred stifles the voice of the conscience and encourages the mind to commit wrongful acts. It justifies harming the innocent. But as hatred cools and perception clears, the mind realizes the wrong it has committed and then feels guilt for what it has done. It feels a guilt that gnaws at its dignity, eats away at its purpose, and pulls it from the straight path. Woe to the mind dominated by hate. Its hatred shall drag it to Hell.

Hatred shall not serve you. An unjust deed committed cannot be undone. Revenge cannot turn back time. It cannot return to you those whom you loved nor that which you lost. For your own sake, treat the wrongdoer justly. Grieve and learn, and if you are strong enough, forgive.

Envy

Envy is to covet what another has and seek to take it, in the belief that the possession of it shall grant happiness.

The envious want their neighbor's house, their neighbor's job, their neighbor's spouse, their neighbor's life. They believe such things shall bring them meaning. They are deluded. Such things shall not make them happy.

Those who continually compare themselves to others can never be fulfilled. The envious have lost sight of their own purpose and hope to take another's purpose. They are deluded. Purpose cannot be stolen. God gave to each soul its own purpose to fulfil and no other.

Pity the envious. The thief gains nothing from what he steals because what he steals is not his. It turns hollow in his grasp and empties him. It distracts him from his purpose. The stolen coin buys only pain.

Pity the envious. Their jealousy arises from unhappiness in not fulfilling their purpose. They are too distracted watching others to see the gifts God has given to them. They need not steal to be happy. God has given to them everything they need to fulfil their purpose and achieve happiness. He has given to them the straight path and the means to walk it. If they listen to their souls, they shall find it.

Those who follow their purpose are never envious of others, for they have discovered happiness. They submit to God's will and by doing so they achieve their purpose. If they need a car to achieve their purpose, they shall get one; if they don't need a car to achieve their purpose, then they won't get one. Material possessions are insignificant. The throat that tastes purpose never thirsts. True wealth lies along the straight path.

Arrogance

Arrogance is ignorance. It is to believe one is better than others. It is to believe that, because one is better than others, one deserves more than others and from this delusion to act unjustly toward others.

The arrogant believe they are better than others because of their money, their appearance, their sex, their race, or their religion. They are wrong. The wealthy are no better than the poor nor the poor better than the wealthy. Brown eyes are no better than blue eyes nor blue eyes better than brown. Men are no better than women nor women better than men. White skin is no better than black skin nor black skin better than white. The believer is no better than the nonbeliever nor the nonbeliever better than the believer. The arrogant are deluded. All humans are equal. Only action separates human from human.

The arrogant lie to themselves. They grasp at certainties founded upon false preconceptions and illusionary absolutes. They grasp at a belief in their own superiority and inherent invulnerability. Their certainty breeds overconfidence and denies an understanding of change. Lacking an understanding of change, they are unable to adapt to change when it occurs. This makes them vulnerable.

The universe is ever changing. The only constants are God and His straight path. Yet the arrogant deny this. They believe they shall never fail. They cling to this belief even as it drags them toward the edge of the abyss. God has set His law. The arrogant shall fall.

Arrogance is a sign of a distracted mind. It is a sign of a mind losing the ability to learn. The mind learns from the mistakes it makes, but arrogance blocks learning because it stops the mind from identifying its mistakes. The arrogant presume they are infallible, that they are beyond the will of God. They make the same mistakes again and again because they cannot see their mistakes. Unable to learn, the arrogant are unable to adapt. And so they eventually fall.

Arrogance inhibits perception. It covers the eyes and blocks the ears. The more arrogant the mind becomes, the less it perceives of the world around it, until it peers through no more than a crack. Eventually, arrogance blocks out everything in the mind except that which strengthens the mind's own preconceived delusions of superiority. It stops the mind from perceiving even that which shall lead to the body's demise. Thus the enslaved have overcome the corrupt when the corrupt have grown complacent, believing the enslaved cannot harm them.

Arrogance leads to laziness, to avoidable errors, and avoidable mistakes. Pity those who allow their arrogance to overcome their judgment. It shall lead to their demise. Arrogance pulls down people, nations, and civilizations. Arrogance renews humanity.

The arrogant act unjustly toward others. They covet their privileged positions and do whatever they can to protect their privileges. They see others as less deserving of just treatment than themselves. They accept the enslavement of others for profit. Arrogance leads to greater sin.

Avoid arrogant thoughts and gestures. Walk meekly in the world and respect those around you. God punishes the complacent and those who believe they are more deserving than others.

Grip humility and take nothing for granted. Avoid the delusion that you are one of God's chosen people. God has no chosen people. His will is the salvation of all of humanity, not just the few.

The virtuous are humble. Do not boast of good deeds nor of avoiding sin. To do so is to make a false god of pride and arrogance.

Beware the blind faith of the arrogant who believe something should happen because they want it to happen. Avoid predicting the future. To do so is folly. Only God knows what shall come. You are a servant of God. Submit to His will, and you shall experience happiness. Follow God's straight path and achieve salvation.

Cowardice

Cowardice is to fear the wrong thing, to fear a thing too much, and to fear a thing at the wrong time. It is to permit fear to gain control over the mind and corrupt the actions of the body. It is to commit wrong instead of right, to reject virtue and follow vice.

It is right to fear what should be feared: the blade and the bullet, the disease and the fire. But it is wrong to fear what should not be feared, what cannot cause harm. It is wrong to fear the different just because it is different or the new just because it is new. This is ignorance. To do so is to feed fear and strengthen fear; it is to drown in fear and make a false god of fear.

It is right to feel fear when faced with danger, for this is the body's natural response to a threat. Fear inspires caution, and caution heightens the body's awareness, which increases the body's ability to avoid danger. However, it is wrong to fear a thing too much. Rather than increasing awareness, too much fear blocks perception. It reduces the body's ability to perceive a threat and respond to it.

It is right to fear at the right time, when a life is threatened or great pain is inflicted. But it is wrong to fear at the wrong time, when there is no danger or danger is far away. This is to fear when there is nothing to fear. To fear when there is nothing to fear is to allow fear to gain control over the mind. The mind must restrain fear as soon as it arises. To not do so is to allow fear to fester and gain greater force. It is to give fear the opportunity to convince the mind that vice is right. Fear breeds fear. Fear feeds apathy, prejudice, and hate.

It is wrong to commit vice to avoid what is feared. Pity the coward who betrays and hurts others to avoid pain, who remains indifferent to the suffering of others and refuses to act when he should. He flees from a bee to be bitten by a snake. He does not understand that the pain of the body is little compared to the pain of the soul. There are worse deaths than the death of the body.

Pity the coward who has grown addicted to fear and has learned to fear everything. He has permitted fear to become the new master of his body and for his mind to become fear's slave. No longer does he control his eyes or his fingers. His eyes cannot look at what he fears. They dart around and refuse to remain steady. His fingers tremble when what he fears draws near. They refuse his commands. He cannot avoid what threatens him because he cannot see it. He cannot ward off what threatens him because he refuses to touch it. So fear threatens his survival because it deprives him of control over the thing that can save him: his body.

Pity the coward. He is blind to what fear takes from him. Fear is the great limiter. It stifles the mind's willingness to seize an opportunity when it is presented. It strangles the mind's initiative. It feeds greedily upon the mind's confidence. And as the mind loses confidence in itself, it loses confidence in its ability to act righteously. Fear convinces the mind that its purpose cannot be achieved. It convinces the mind that it cannot act, so it refuses to act. Fear is the greatest thief, for it steals the mind's most precious possession: the straight path.

Resist the corrupt who rob the mind of courage and infect it with fear; who steal the mind's capacity to act; who steal from the mind the straight path. They spread fear to enslave the weak and the innocent. Woe to the corrupt who corrupt others. Woe to the corrupt who make the straight path crooked. They shall not escape God's justice.

Wisdom is the proper weighing of things. Devote your life to the great things and avoid being distracted by the little things. Worry not whether you shall have clothes to wear, food to eat, or water to drink. Life is more important than these. The body can be fully clothed and still be naked, full of food and drink and still be starving. Its greatest need is God. First seek the straight path, then lesser things shall follow. God provides the righteous with all they need to fulfil His will.

Retain your dignity and be brave. Birth and death are the most profound experiences of life. A baby is born calm or angry but never cringing or fearful. He is born with dignity. And when death draws near, a human should die with dignity: angry or calm, yes, but never sobbing or fearful. We learn fear; we are not born with it. Fear is an emotion of the body, not of the soul. Mimic the baby. Die with dignity and strive for a noble death.

Lust

Lust is to be overwhelmed by sexual desire for another and to act to satisfy that desire. It is to seek pleasure and submit to pleasure. It is to put pleasure before love and put the body before the mind. It is to revel in vice and forget the soul.

Woe to the lustful whose minds are enslaved by desire. They kneel at the feet of their obsession and have made a false god of their lust. Lust dominates their thoughts and acts. It chains their eyes to the object of their desire and binds their fingers to its touch. It compels them to think of sex and ignore other thoughts. It distracts them. And when the object of their desire is denied, lust stokes their anger.

Woe to the lustful who turn to pornography to satisfy their need. They buy images to satisfy their appetite, but one image is never enough to sate lust. Lust is a greedy master and can never be sated. It always hungers for more.

Pity those addicted to lust. Pity those robbed of their freedom. The more they submit to lust, the greater hold lust takes of their minds. It always demands their attention. It pesters them and robs them of calm. It compels them to perform lewd acts and chips away at their dignity and their sense of self-worth. It makes them slaves to the purveyor of images, slaves to the corrupt.

Better to lead a chaste life than become a slave. For chastity and love free the mind from lust and from the manipulations of the corrupt. Ever the corrupt seek profit. Greed is their god.

Lust is an addiction. Addiction is a compulsion to satisfy desire. It is evil because it enslaves the mind. It chains the mind to the body and weakens the mind's authority over the body. It makes the body master of the mind.

Addiction drains the mind's willpower. A mind bereft of willpower no longer hears its soul. A mind bereft of willpower cannot complete its purpose and walk the straight path.

Pity those trapped by addiction, who look for happiness but cannot see it, who stumble into addiction to gain a brief respite from pain. Pity those who have lost their way.

No addict deserves their addiction. Lust cannot satisfy the mind nor the body. Sea water cannot quench thirst. Pity the innocent who stumble into Hell. May they find the straight path again and enter Heaven.

God drives humanity's evolution. He demands that we improve ourselves and strengthen our minds and bodies so that we survive and prosper. Addiction weakens the mind and the body. It retards humanity's evolution. Addiction is a sin, for it denies God's will.

God despises those who addict others for profit. To addict an adult is evil, to addict a child is abomination. Woe to the corrupt who steal a child's innocence. Hell awaits them.

God despises a society that addicts its people for profit. Such a society is dying, for it no longer loves its people. It wants to weaken its people and exploit them rather than strengthen them. It is a diseased corpse. God's justice shall cleanse the corpse from this Earth.

Do not confuse lust with love. Love is infinite, while lust is finite. Love endures where lust fades. Love is happy with the object of its love. Lust tires with the object of its desire and seeks ever anew to satisfy its appetite. Love grows stronger with each passing moment and gives joy to the mind and strengthens the body. Lust grows weaker with each passing moment and angers the mind and weakens the body. Love is unselfish. The stronger it grows, the more it places the good of the person it loves before its own. Lust is selfish. It cares only for satisfying its own appetite and nothing for the object of its desire. Blessed are the lovers. Their love strengthens humanity. Their love pleases God.

Greed

Greed is to yearn for material things and devote one's life to the accumulation of those things. It is to desire more than others have and to take from others to satisfy that desire. It is to be distracted by the insignificant. It is to put aside the riches of Heaven for the baubles of Earth. It is to reject the straight path.

Greed is the improper weighing of things. It is ignorance. The greedy gather dust and cup it in their hands. They count the specks and reach down to pick up more, all the time unaware of the specks falling through their fingers. They believe they can hold onto dust forever. They believe there is no wind. They lie to themselves. A wish won't hold back the wind. God's wind brings wisdom.

The greedy hoard the things of the world. They gather coins to buy delicious foods, expensive homes, and beautiful people. With each new purchase, their body rewards them with a moment of pleasure. They buy more and more to experience more pleasure. Yet their pleasure gives them no happiness or satisfaction. For the things that they buy cannot fulfil their purpose. A mountain of gold cannot buy a single step on the straight path.

The greedy revel in luxurious things. They delight in the taste of rich foods and the touch of expensive fabrics. They indulge in precious objects and pursue wealth with all their thought. And in so doing, they no longer gain joy from the gifts that God has given to them. They no longer see God's love. The more the eye looks for money, the more money becomes the only thing the eye can see. The greedy forget their soul and see only the sparkle of gold.

Greed weakens the body. The trays of chocolates and mounds of meat make the body fat and slow. The fluffy cushions and silk sheets make the body soft. The idle time and expensive entertainments make the body lazy. And all these greedy things compel the body to seek more. All these greedy things consume the will and take away the body's capacity to adapt to hardship and learn God's lessons.

Money is just paper, plastic, and metal. It is neither good nor evil, as the knife is neither good nor evil. It is simply a tool to be used to achieve a goal. Much can be achieved with wealth when used properly, to help others and rectify injustice. But wealth becomes worthless when used unjustly to weaken others.

Great indeed is the temptation of gold. Pity the greedy, for they succumb to temptation. They choose to place coin before righteousness. They take from others and say wrong is right. God knows all lies. Take nothing from another. Only the thief steals from others.

Greed withers compassion. Woe to the tightfisted who turn away the helpless knocking at their door. Woe to the tightfisted who refuse to spend a few coins to feed the hungry beggar. Truly the beggar is God's witness! Pity those who have made a false god of greed and have chosen to bow at the feet of Mammon. They have chosen the wrong path. One cannot serve two masters. God is not unjust to the greedy. The greedy are unjust to themselves.

Righteousness purifies wealth. Blessed are the generous who give their own to help others in need. Their wealth shall be returned to them tenfold. To give one coin to a beggar is to give ten coins to the soul.

Woe to the manufacturers of greed. Woe to the corrupt who enslave others for profit, who make others greedy so as to profit from their greed. Woe to the corrupt who turn an innocent human into a worker-consumer, who works to consume and whose consumption forces him to work. Woe to the corrupt who, to feed their own appetites, rob others of their independence; who turn others into cows content to eat grass. Woe to the corrupt who make the straight path crooked. They shall be punished with a scourge. Their gold shall drag them to Hell.

Sloth

Sloth is to avoid exerting the mind and the body. It is to weaken the mind's authority over the body. It is to hide from struggle and to submit rather than resist. It is to take the easy way rather than the hard. It is to ignore purpose and step from the straight path.

Sloth is laziness. The lazy man sins against himself. He refuses to learn how to grow wheat, ford the river, and climb the mountain. He refuses to perform acts that require an effort. He hides from struggle and denies himself the rewards that come from struggle. Struggle strengthens the mind and the body.

Sloth slows the body's thoughts and movements. The lazy man refuses to exercise his body, so his bones grow brittle and his muscles grow soft. He refuses to exert his will, so the authority of his mind over his body diminishes. He refuses to heed his conscience and listen to his soul, so he forgets truth. He prefers instead to remain on the couch. Sloth drinks the body's life.

The lazy man confuses the easy with the hard. Every time he retreats from an obstacle and rejects the opportunity to strengthen his mind and body, he adds another stone to the wall that stands between him and his purpose. Sloth denies him the straight path.

The lazy man grows apathetic. He refuses to struggle because he believes struggle is futile. So he accepts his own suffering and the suffering of others. He witnesses the abuse of children and says nothing. He remains silent in the face of injustice. He refuses to heed God's will and protect the weak. Apathy is the haven of the coward.

Pity the lazy man who refuses to act righteously. He accepts vice and is thus tainted by vice. The corrupt and the silent share the same fate.

Avoid confusing sloth with rest. God condemns the first and welcomes the second. Sloth is to waste time and weaken the body. Rest is to regain strength after a struggle undertaken and a purpose fulfilled. It is reward for righteous action. Strive for five days and rest for two.

The body needs to rest and sleep. It cannot walk forever. During the journey, it must sit down and appreciate the clouds and the trees. It must take time to love family and enjoy friendship. It must celebrate the events that deserve celebration, the births, the marriages, and the deaths. It must commemorate and honor the righteous deeds of others. It must enjoy God's creation and take time to stop and listen. An exhausted body cannot hear the mind and the soul.

Sloth creates errors and mistakes. The lazy man lacks the will to complete tasks properly and leaves it to others to fix his mistakes. He wastes others' time and endangers those who rely upon him. He refuses to tie a rope tightly, so it comes undone and others fall. He nails one nail into a boat instead of two, so the boat breaks apart and others drown. The lazy knot loosens, the lazy board breaks. Sloth endangers life.

Pity the lazy man who cannot be trusted to complete a task properly. He is unreliable and loses his friends because he loses their respect and trust. Pity the lazy man left alone to wallow in sloth. He has been deprived of the means to escape vice. It is easier to conquer vice with the help of others than alone. It is easier to climb over a wall with a ladder. God helps those who help each other.

Avoid television. Television is a distraction. It is the breeder of sloth. It teaches the body nothing except how to press the on button and watch a screen. Watching another climb a mountain on television does not teach the mind and the body how to climb a mountain. The mountain must be climbed to learn how to climb it. Only then shall the fingers and the toes learn how to find the cracks, and the muscles of the arms and legs grow strong enough to lift the torso. Experience brings knowledge.

Television takes from the innocent and gives to the greedy. The greedy use television to sell their products and spread the lie that consumption is purpose. They use television to compel the innocent to consume things they do not need. They use television to persuade the innocent to succumb to greed. They use television to steal from the innocent and turn them into slaves. Television distracts the mind and the body from the straight path.

Television is a drug. It is addictive because it creates a need in the body to watch it more. It compels the eyes to watch the screen. It weakens the muscles and dissipates the will. It turns humans into cows. Why is a cow fat and lazy? Because it stands in a field eating grass all day. Pity those who become cows. May God save them. May God take them from the field and place them at the foot of the mountain.

Remember compassion and beware judging others. Forgive the lazy man. Vice has trapped him. He is lost and distracted, unaware of his error. He questions his own abilities and refuses to strengthen himself because he believes he cannot strengthen himself. Pity those who have allowed sloth to feast upon their confidence.

Many a body has fallen to sloth through no fault of its own. Pity the child who has been surrounded by messages of sloth and conditioned to laziness from birth. Pity the child who has been made to watch the television and the tablet, and as a result of watching these objects, has lost the ability to concentrate and to see and hear clearly.

Pity the child who has been fed foods to fatten him, who has been given tools to weaken him by making his life "easier." Beware the tool. Be certain it gives more than it takes.

Great is God's love and compassion. He witnesses the lazy and sends the righteous to help them. He sends the righteous to awaken the lazy and remind them of their purpose; to help them once again see the straight path.

Beware the errors of sloth. Seek right and reject wrong. Act righteously and complete tasks properly. If something falls from its proper place, then raise it up again. If a thing is dangerous, then make it safe. To leave a task unfinished is to see it fail in the future.

God gives this task to you and no other. It is for you alone to complete. If you cannot complete the small tasks God gives to you, then you shall be unable to complete the great ones He gives to you later.

Each moment is precious, for it has been given to you by God. So avoid wasting time. Use your time wisely out of respect for yourself and God. To waste time is to waste life.

When your body dies, you shall judge your actions, not God. You shall judge whether you fulfilled your duty. You shall judge whether you helped others when you should have and used the time God gave to you to strengthen your mind and body. The mind cannot hide from itself.

☞ Book 3 ☜

The Body

I. The Body

God drew the body from the mind as He drew the mind
from the soul. He fashioned the body with nerve, muscle, blood, and bone and enclosed it in skin. He then
gave to the body senses to perceive what was around it,
to strengthen it, and to protect it.

God created the body as a tool for the soul to aid the
soul in its exploration of the universe. He gave the body
to the soul so the soul could learn about, share with, and
touch the universe. He gave the body to the soul so the
pure could touch the impure.

The soul wears the body as the hand does the glove.
It has worn many gloves during its journey and it shall
wear many more, for the soul endures when the body
decays. The body grows and lives and passes away and
encases what it learns in the bodies it conceives. It shares
with other bodies so all can evolve and fulfil God's will.

Like the sculptor does the clay, the soul chooses the
body that best suits its purpose. It directs the body toward
virtue and away from vice so that the body is strengthened rather than weakened. And as the body evolves, it

becomes better able to follow the commands of the soul and walk the straight path. Blessed is the body that submits to the commands of the soul. It shall have joy in this life and the life to come.

At birth, the body is both empty and full: empty of experiences from its life yet to be lived and full of the memories of its ancestors. It is empty of experience, so it yearns to learn and acts to strengthen itself. It is full of the memories of its ancestors, so it can add to what they have achieved.

Deep is the well of ancestral memory, a well the body drinks from in times of need but must hide from itself so as not to drown, for the body is not the soul and can be aware of only so much.

One body has a thousand parents: its parents, their parents, and their parents before them. It is a link in an ever-burgeoning chain, each link stronger than the last. In each cell of the body swims the knowledge gained by all its ancestors. And the body in turn passes on what it has learned to its children. Nothing is lost or wasted. Great is the reward of a skill attained, for once it is learned it is passed down the chain.

Woe to the body that revels in vice. Woe to the body that refuses to heed the commands of the soul. It shall grow brittle like a rusty link in a chain. And if the bodies that it conceives continue to wallow in vice, then the chain shall break. Woe to those who sin against themselves, for they sin against their children. Blessed are those who act righteously, for they reward themselves and their children to come.

Body follows body. The body is constantly learning and evolving; strengthening itself through its actions, adapting to its environment, and shaping itself in response to the thoughts of the mind; always reinforcing the strengths and dampening the weaknesses of its parents. It exerts itself to grow stronger so its senses sharpen, its limbs grow more agile, and the voice of the soul grows clearer. Blessed are those who quicken their own evolution. They are servants of God.

II.   Discipline

The body is the tool of the soul. And like a tool, it must be sharpened and hardened to achieve its purpose: this is achieved through discipline. Discipline is the imposition of the will of the mind upon the flesh of the body. It is to shape the body through conscious thought and action.

Discipline establishes the proper relationship between the soul, the mind, and the body. It teaches the body to submit to the commands of the mind and strengthens the mind's authority over the body. It gives the mind the strength to control lethargy and frustration, pain and fear. It gives the body the strength to meet God's tests and overcome them.

The body can achieve nothing without discipline. It cannot learn to write nor speak the truth, to overcome an obstacle nor complete the final step of a journey. Only a disciplined body can achieve its purpose. Only a disciplined body can pursue virtue and reject vice. And only a disciplined body can walk the straight path and fulfil the will of God.

For the disciplined body, the straight path is only one step ahead, but for the undisciplined body, the straight path lies beyond the horizon.

III. Mental Conditioning

The body achieves discipline through mental and physical conditioning. One cannot exist without the other. There can be no mental conditioning without physical conditioning, and there can be no physical conditioning without mental conditioning. Each relies upon the other and fortifies the other. Every conscious act to condition and strengthen the body is a step toward the straight path.

The aim of mental conditioning is to gain greater control over thought. Uncontrolled thoughts are slippery fish. They dart this way and that to avoid the mind's grip, seeking instead the random currents of bodily desire. They are wasted thoughts, as they refuse to fulfil their purpose: to direct the body to strengthen itself and walk the straight path.

Only controlled thought strengthens the body. And controlled thought can be attained only through mental conditioning. Mental conditioning strengthens the mind's authority over the body and disciplines thought so as to protect the body against vice. It submits the body to the will.

There are four kinds of mental conditioning: meditation, fasting, prayer, and learning. They must all be practiced to discipline the body.

Meditation

The first kind of mental conditioning is meditation. Meditation is to free the mind from the distraction of bodily desire and strengthen the mind's control over thought.

The goal of meditation is to give the mind greater control over the brain. The brain develops the habit of thinking for the sake of thinking without considering why it thinks the thoughts it does. This is a difficult habit to break. Such a brain is occupied by random thoughts that create a constant chatter. This chatter distracts the mind and is difficult for the soul to pierce. It blocks the mind from hearing the soul.

Meditation enables the mind to control the brain and reassert its authority over the body. By willing the brain not to think, silence is achieved and the voice of the soul can be heard. The soul speaks only to the mind prepared to assume its proper authority over the body.

The brain is a muscle like any other, and like other muscles it must be trained and strengthened, otherwise it atrophies. Meditation achieves this. It gives to the mind greater control over the thoughts that course through the brain. It aids clear thinking. It expands and deepens the perception of the senses—improving sight, hearing, taste, smell, and touch. It enables the mind to tap the innate abilities of the body. It opens the eyes to the light surrounding other bodies and the skin to the ghost wind. It thrusts perception outward to experience the realm of the spirit.

The mind needs to practice regularly to meditate properly. In the beginning, meditation is hard, but it grows easier over time. Do not expect immediate results. The fingers cannot learn to play the piano in a day. It is the same with meditation. Practicing once a year achieves nothing. The mind can only learn how to meditate by practicing daily.

Meditation requires solitude. Find a quiet place free from the distractions of the world. Relax the body by sitting or lying down. Remove all stress from the muscles. This helps the mind to focus its attention. As the muscles

The Body   57

relax, they shall ache and itch. Ignore this, for it is the body trying to draw the mind's attention back to the body.

Next, focus the mind's attention on one thing and nothing. Stare at a point in the dark, and allow the eyes to lose focus on the point without loosening the mind's attention upon the point. The brain shall to try to distract the mind again, for the brain is made to think. It shall create distracting thoughts from habit. It shall drag up memories or create an itch in the toe or nose to draw the mind's attention back to itself. Sometimes other things appear or are sensed. Ignore these, too. If the mind focuses upon a distraction, its attention shall waver and the meditation shall fail.

As the mind draws its attention away from the body and toward itself, the body's breathing slows and grows shallower until it is noticed little. The muscles relax further and grow heavier. Then the presence of the muscles and flesh recedes. This is the consciousness passing from the body to the mind. With this passing comes clarity, strength, and a reawakening of purpose.

Fasting

The second kind of mental conditioning is fasting. The aim of fasting is to gain greater authority over the body so that the mind can hear the voice of the soul more clearly and respond to its commands.

Fasting is effective only when the body and the mind fast in unison, when the body rejects the object and the mind rejects the desire to obtain that object. If the mind refuses to think about drinking alcohol, then the body shall refuse to drink alcohol. If the mind thinks about drinking alcohol, then the body shall drink alcohol. Block the desire so as to block the action.

There is mental fasting and physical fasting. Mental fasting is to restrain the mind from thinking wrong thoughts. Physical fasting is to restrain the body from eating meat or drinking alcohol and from performing sexual acts. Mental fasting cleanses thought, and physical fasting cleanses the blood, flesh, and organs. The mind suffers less from the fear and pain experienced by the body the more it establishes its authority over the body.

Blessed is he who can control his desires and thus control himself. He has disciplined his mind and body.

Prayer

The third kind of mental conditioning is prayer. Prayer is performed to honor God and to ask guidance from God during times of need. It shifts the mind's attention away from the distractions of the body and toward the soul and its purpose. It strengthens the connection between the mind, the soul, and God.

To pray is to communicate with God. It requires discipline and the utmost respect and reverence from the mind and the body. Before prayer, wash the body and don clean clothes. Be free of all thoughts of lust, envy, greed, and hate. To bring vice to God is to disrespect God and dishonor oneself in the face of God. The selfish prayer is dust in the wind.

When praying, place both hands in front of the body, the left palm against the right. Straighten the fingers, each finger next to the other and all pointing upwards. Bow the head and close the eyes.

Pray once a day and begin with the "Prayer of the Straight Path":

Almighty God
My savior and my guide
Grant me the strength
To walk Your straight path
To seek virtue and to reject vice
To discipline my body and my mind
And to strengthen myself
So I strengthen humankind.

By praying once a day, the mind is reminded of its soul and God. It is also reminded of its purpose: to walk the straight path. The mind that prays once a day shall seek virtue and reject vice.

To pray with others is called a guidance. Pray with others when possible, for prayer gives comfort and support to others and to those who no longer see the truth. Through prayer, those who walk the straight path shall help others to find the straight path again. This pleases God, for God helps those who help each other.

When possible, seek a holy place to pray. Seek a place free of vice: a temple or a church, a beach or a meadow. Vice stains all it touches, be it a body or a stone, and distracts the mind when it can. But if a holy place cannot be found, then fall to both knees and pray. Ask and God shall give. Speak the truth and God shall hear. Even Hell cannot hide the truth from God.

Learning

The fourth kind of mental conditioning is learning. Only through learning can the mind and the body overcome mistakes. Only through learning can they begin to understand God's creation and achieve the purpose God has set for them.

Learning begins with two lessons. The first lesson to learn is that God created the mind to learn. The second lesson to learn is that the mind can learn. These are the most important, yet, for some minds, the most difficult of lessons. Once the mind has learned these lessons, then all other lessons become easy.

Seek to learn a new thing each day, be it a new word, a new skill, or how to perform a task better. To refuse to learn is to stagnate and retard the evolution of the mind and the body.

Seek knowledge from an expert rather than a novice, as an expert understands how to properly teach a skill, for he has learned that skill himself. To learn about chemistry, seek a chemist; to learn about farming, seek a farmer. The wise seek knowledge from the wise. Fools seek knowledge from the ignorant.

Seek knowledge from elders. Elders have learned much from their experiences. They are wise and want to pass their knowledge on to the young so that the young learn and can avoid the same mistakes that the elders made. Elders yearn to strengthen humanity. Only the fool rejects an expert and turns his back on wisdom.

Learning strengthens the mind and the body. At birth, the body contains only a few memories of its present life, but it is full of ancestral memories. Learning is a process of meshing the knowledge from these ancestral memories with the knowledge gained from new experiences.

When a baby begins to walk, he concentrates on placing one foot in front of the other while maintaining his balance with his arms and torso. He learns much from observing his parents and other people walking around him. Yet this is not his only source of knowledge. When he begins to walk, he also begins to remember how to walk.

Each cell of his body contains memories of his ancestors walking. These memories whisper to him, reminding him and directing him to reclaim and improve upon his innate abilities. They direct the growth of his torso, his hands and his arms, his feet and his legs. They fashion his body to walk upright on two legs. His legs know how to walk. They just need to be reminded of their purpose.

Each of us is an individual and a community, a single consciousness and a vessel cradling the memories and experiences of our ancestors. Our purpose is to learn more so as to strengthen ourselves, to add to the knowledge inherited from our ancestors, and to pass this knowledge to our descendants. Our purpose is to make our children stronger, quicker, and smarter than we are so that they can hear their souls more clearly and are better able to walk the straight path. Our purpose is to continue and quicken our evolution so that humanity survives.

IV. Physical Conditioning

The organs, muscles, bones, and senses grow in response to the actions of the body. They are strengthened when challenged and weakened when not. The eye that refuses to see shall lose its sight, the ear that refuses to listen shall lose its hearing, and the leg that refuses to walk shall go lame.

Pity the worker who sits at a desk all day staring at a screen. His muscles atrophy and his sight grows dim. He becomes an old man at thirty-six. Pity those who forget their purpose. May they rediscover their purpose and walk the straight path.

Physical conditioning strengthens the body by submitting the body to the mind and thus the soul. It disciplines the body and gives to the body the strength the body needs to follow the commands of the soul and walk the straight path.

To discipline the body, each part of the body is conditioned in turn: the eye, the ear, the mouth, the nose, the hand, the foot, and the torso. And each part of the body is conditioned, not to make it stronger than another body but to make it stronger than it was before. God has given to each soul the responsibility to strengthen its own body and no other.

Have faith in God and yourself. He has given you the strength to condition your body and to learn about the universe. Do what can be done. Begin walking slowly and rest when necessary. If taking three steps is too difficult, then take two. If taking two steps is too difficult, then take one. The more steps taken, the easier they become. Fear only inaction and persevere, as the reward is great. For each conscious act to strengthen the body is a step closer toward the straight path.

The Eye

God created the eye to evolve. He created the eye to improve the mind's perception and understanding of the body's surroundings. He created the eye to help the mind to walk the straight path.

The eye must be conditioned to strengthen its sight. It is conditioned through the conscious direction of the mind. The mind conditions the eye by directing the eye toward what strengthens its sight and by guiding the eye away from what weakens its sight. The eye that refuses to look near shall no longer see near. The eye that refuses to look far shall no longer see far.

The eye must be conditioned to see clearly, refreshed or exhausted, certain or afraid. It must be conditioned to see near, to spot a tick on a leaf or a fleck of gold in the sand. It must be conditioned to see far, to spot a circling eagle in the sky or a boat on the horizon. It must be conditioned to follow and anticipate the movement of things, to track the path of a fish in a river or the line of a falling rock. It must be conditioned to hold multiple things within its vision, to see one detail amongst many and many details amongst one, to see a stone in a desert of stones and at the same time identify the color, ridges, and shape of that stone. And it must be conditioned to perceive the proper weight of things, to distinguish the important from the unimportant.

The eye must hold its gaze steady when the body is tested to see clearly. It must hold its gaze steady when the body is exhausted after walking for days or when the body stands within a sandstorm or a gale. It must hold its gaze steady when confronted by fear and other emotions that try to cloud its sight. It should never divert its gaze, as this endangers the body. Better to see a thing so as to meet it or avoid it. The eye sees more clearly when its lids are open, when the forehead is free of wrinkles and when the mind is calm and free of distraction. This is the proper gaze for the eye.

The eye must observe those things close to it to see near. It must observe surrounding objects and learn the appearance of those objects. It must step from the room and walk into the forest. It must learn the appearance of leaves and trees, rocks and water; and it must learn to perceive their various states, to distinguish a healthy tree from a diseased tree and recognize the cause of the disease.

The eye must look into the distance to see far. It must go to places where it is compelled to look far and avoid places where it is forced to stare down at the ground. It must look to the birds in the sky to discover a source of water. It must climb to the top of the mountain and look down into the valley to see where the path leads. It must look up to the stars to know north from south and distinguish the right direction from the wrong direction.

The eye must look at moving objects and act in unison with the hands, the feet, and other parts of the body to improve its perception of speed and distance. When the eye observes the hand catching a stick and throwing a stick, then the eye learns the time it takes for a stick to move from one point to another. When the eye observes the foot receiving a ball and kicking a ball, then the eye learns the time it takes for a ball to move from one point to another. The more the eye watches the hand throwing an object and the foot kicking an object, the better the eye's awareness of speed and distance becomes.

The eye must expand the scope of its vision to see multiple things at the same time. The eye's vision expands when it and the body are free of distraction. The mind sees all the eye sees when the eye is calm but little when the eye is distracted. The more things the eye permits the mind to see, the more the mind knows and the better the mind is able to direct the eye toward what is significant. The calm eye sees the bark of a tree, a bee on a flower, and, if it needs to, a spider on a branch.

The eye must look many places to strengthen its sight. It must avoid staring at the same point for long periods of time. It must avoid staring at a computer or television screen for hours each day. This weakens the eye.

The eye must study what others have learned to perceive the proper weight of things. It must study religion to see the inner truth of things, to remember the straight path and learn about the nature of God's creation. It must study the history of animals and humans to see the causes of things, to understand why some things have prospered and others have failed. And it must study science to see the outer shell of things, to understand their outer nature and increase the mind's ability to learn about and adapt to the universe.

The eye must perform actions such as these until the mind no longer needs to guide the eye toward what strengthens it and away from what weakens it. The eye must perform these actions until it guides itself. Once the eye watches what strengthens it and avoids what weakens it without the guidance of the mind and conscious thought, then it is disciplined.

The Ear

God created the ear to evolve. He created the ear to increase the mind's perception and understanding of the body's surroundings and to allow the mind to perceive through hearing what it cannot perceive through sight. He created the ear so the mind can know what lies around the corner before it comes into view. If the mind relies only upon what the eye sees, then its other senses weaken.

The ear must be conditioned to strengthen its hearing. It is conditioned through the conscious direction of the mind. The mind conditions the ear by encouraging the ear to listen to sounds that strengthen its hearing and by guiding the ear away from sounds that weaken its hearing.

Pity the ear that listens only to its headphones. It weakens itself. It refuses to listen to the sounds surrounding it, so it is unable to recognize those sounds. It fails to learn the difference between the sound of an oasis and the sound of an abattoir. Listen only to headphones, and only headphones shall you hear. The ear that refuses to listen shall fall deaf.

The ear must be conditioned to hear loud sounds and faint sounds. It must be conditioned to hear moving sounds. It must be conditioned to hear one sound amongst many and many sounds amongst one. And it must be conditioned to hear when a voice speaks the truth or a lie.

The ear must listen to loud sounds to recognize loud sounds. Loud sounds tell the ear much. They announce salvation and warn of danger. The ear must listen to a firecracker exploding and a gun shooting to learn the difference between the sounds these objects make. The more the ear listens to these sounds, the better the ear shall know the presence of a firecracker or a gun without having to see them, and the better the ear shall perceive when a weapon is near and help the body to avoid it.

The ear must listen to faint sounds to recognize faint sounds. It must listen to the sound of water trickling down a stream and a breeze blowing through trees to tell the difference between the sound of water rushing and leaves rustling. When the ear knows these sounds, it can recognize when water is near to quench the body's thirst.

The ear must listen to moving sounds to know the proximity of a thing. It must go to a forest and listen to the sound of a foot crunching leaves and of a body brushing against twigs and branches to distinguish the sound of a human walking through a forest from that of an animal, and to know where that human or animal is located in the forest. The more the ear listens to moving sounds, the better it is able to identify the proximity of the things creating those sounds without having to see them.

The ear must listen to different sounds to recognize one sound amongst many and many sounds amongst one. The more sounds the ear hears, the more sounds it learns, and the more sounds it learns in combination with other sounds, the better the ear can hear those combinations of sounds. The more the ear listens at the same time to the dull rumble of a plane in the sky, to the voice of a person walking by, and to the creak of floorboards in an adjoining room, the quicker the ear learns which way the plane is flying, what the person is saying, and who is standing on the other side of the door. The ear that recognizes one sound amongst many and many sounds amongst one tells the mind what surrounds the body. This strengthens the mind by increasing its perception.

The ear must listen to spoken words to learn when a voice tells the truth or a lie. It must seek out the honest and the dishonest, the martyr and the thief, and listen to the words they speak. Words come from the mind. They are born from reason and emotion. The ear that listens to words learns to hear both the reasons and the emotions shaping those words, and from considering both, learns how to distinguish the truth from a lie.

A liar's body tells his lie. He tries to hide his lie by feigning ease or innocence, but his body betrays him. His muscles twitch or he scratches an itch. His voice sounds unnatural, too uncertain or too jovial, too relaxed or too controlled. This tension in his body is caused by his soul.

The soul hates lies because lies obstruct the will of God. When the body lies, the soul expresses its anger in the body. It tightens the body's muscles and drains the body's energies. It distorts the voice by twisting the lips, tying the tongue, and constricting the throat. The soul makes certain the body cannot hide its lie and the conditioned ear shall hear the lie.

The ear must devote time each day to just listening to further sharpen its hearing. The body must find a place free of distraction where the mind can ignore what the other senses perceive and instead focus only on the sounds the ear hears. This strengthens the ear's hearing, further enhancing the ear's ability to recognize different sounds.

The ear must perform actions such as these until the mind no longer needs to guide the ear toward sounds that strengthen it and away from sounds that weaken it. The ear must listen to these sounds until it guides itself. Once the ear listens to sounds that strengthen it and avoids sounds that weaken it without the guidance of the mind and conscious thought, then it is disciplined. Only then can the ear help the mind to walk the straight path.

The Mouth

God created the mouth to evolve. He created the mouth to add to what the other senses perceive and increase the mind's perception and understanding of the body's surroundings. He created the mouth to enable the mind to express and share its thoughts with others so as to strengthen itself and others. He created the mouth to help the mind to spread the Word of God and remind others of the straight path.

The mouth must be conditioned to strengthen its taste and voice. It must be conditioned to eat fresh food and different foods to increase its sensitivity. It must be conditioned to persuade others by speaking in an appropriate tone, expressing the ideas of the mind with precision, and speaking the truth. It must be conditioned to help others to learn more and walk the straight path.

The mouth is conditioned through the conscious direction of the mind. The mind conditions the mouth by guiding the mouth toward what strengthens its taste and voice, and away from what weakens its taste and voice.

The mouth must eat fresh food to strengthen its taste. It must eat fruit, vegetables, grains, fish, and meat to encourage the growth of its taste buds. As its taste buds grow, the mouth grows more sensitive, enabling it to taste more. It learns how to distinguish fresh food from stale food; it becomes accustomed to eating fresh food, because fresh food tastes better and makes the body feel better. Fresh food is healthy food. It encourages the growth of the nerves, organs, muscles, and bones. Fresh food strengthens the body.

The mouth must eat and drink different types of food and liquid to increase its sensitivity. It must taste tarragon and thyme, chili and salt to understand how these spices and herbs flavor food and to identify their presence in food. It must combine what it tastes with what the nose smells to enhance its taste further. By doing this, it learns the taste of different ingredients and whether these ingredients shall strengthen the body or cause it harm.

The mouth must avoid eating stale food, fast food, and genetically modified food, as these weaken the body. Eating stale food weakens the body because stale food lacks nutrients and contains harmful bacteria. Eating fast food weakens the body because fast food contains excessive amounts of salt, sugar, and fats that damage the body. Eating genetically modified food weakens the body because genetically modified food contains harmful proteins. Genetically modified food has been developed to increase the amount a fruit, vegetable, or grain produces or to increase the resistance of a fruit, vegetable, or grain to weed-killing pesticides. It has been developed to increase the profit gained from selling food rather than to strengthen the body. Genetically modified food is corrupt.

The mouth must avoid consuming addictive substances, as they damage the mouth's sensitivity. Tobacco and other addictive substances weaken the mouth's taste and reduce the mouth's ability to distinguish healthy food from unhealthy food. The mouth robbed of its taste is unable to strengthen the body.

The mouth must be able to persuade others to strengthen its voice. To persuade others, it must learn how to use an appropriate tone, express ideas with precision, and speak the truth. It must be relaxed to speak with an appropriate tone so that the voice is clear. It must avoid grimacing or pouting, as these are signs of a mind distracted by hate and self-obsession. It must know different tones and when to use them. It must speak in a sympathetic tone to comfort others. And it must speak in a commanding tone to lead others.

The mind can understand a thing only once it has experienced that thing. To taste an orange is to understand the taste of an orange. To suffer is to understand suffering. The mind can know the suffering of others only if it has also suffered. Once the mind understands suffering, then the mouth can speak in a sympathetic tone to those who suffer and help them.

It is right to help those who suffer. We share their suffering and ease their pain by showing them sympathy. Sympathy increases trust and respect between people and strengthens the bonds of friendship that they share. It increases the cohesion of a group and the loyalty of its members. It encourages people to help one another and struggle together during times of adversity. God helps those who help one another.

The mouth must speak in a commanding tone when leading others. It must lead small groups, then large groups to develop a commanding tone. It must debate a position and present to an audience, organize a project, and guide a community. This experience strengthens the vocal cords, sharpens the voice, and develops the mind's composure under pressure. It gives the mouth greater confidence and authority. It teaches the mouth how to reason and persuade others and to effectively lead a group to achieve its goals.

The mouth must learn the proper meaning of words to express ideas with precision. It must accurately describe a thing, a feeling, a cause, or a reason. It must speak clear and concise words that convey meaning accurately rather than convoluted words and phrases that sound important but do more to obscure the thoughts of the mind than reveal them. Cost-cutting means firing workers. Collateral damage means killing innocent people. Call a truth a truth and a lie a lie, for that is what they are. Simple words tell truths.

The mouth must speak the truth to strengthen its voice and persuade others. The more the mouth speaks the truth, the more truth binds the mouth, and the more difficult it is for the mouth to tell a lie. Make truth a habit.

But if the mouth tells a lie, then it must admit the lie to free itself of the lie. This strengthens the mouth. God blesses the repentant. Only by using the appropriate tone, expressing ideas with precision, and speaking the truth can the mouth persuade one person or a multitude.

The mouth must perform actions such as these until the mind no longer needs to guide the mouth toward what strengthens it and away from what weakens it. The mouth must perform these actions until it guides itself. Once the mouth eats what strengthens it and avoids what weakens it, speaks the truth and avoids lies, without the guidance of the mind and conscious thought, then it is disciplined. The mouth is disciplined once it spreads the Word of God and reminds others of the straight path.

The Nose

God created the nose to evolve. He created the nose to enhance the mind's perception so the mind can identify the scents and odors that surround the body. He created the nose so the mind can perceive what the eye cannot see, the ear cannot hear, and the mouth cannot taste. Only the nose can smell an island beyond the horizon.

The mind must heed what the nose smells and not just rely upon what the eye sees or the ear hears. God created the nose to protect the body and enable the mind to perceive more of the universe.

The nose must be conditioned to strengthen its sense of smell. It is conditioned through the conscious direction of the mind. The mind conditions the nose by directing the nose toward scents and odors that strengthen its sense of smell and by guiding the nose away from scents and odors that weaken its sense of smell.

The nose must be conditioned to recognize what benefits and harms the body. It must be conditioned to identify one smell amongst many and many smells amongst one, to identify people by their scent and to smell their emotions.

The nose must smell different scents and odors to recognize what benefits and harms the body. It must learn the smell of healthy foods and liquids that strengthen the body so that the body can recognize healthy foods and liquids and consume them. And it must learn the smell of drugs and poisons that harm the body so the body can recognize these substances and avoid them.

Opium enslaves the mind; tobacco burns the nose and the lungs. The body must avoid addicting itself to drugs that weaken the mind and the body and reduce the nose's sensitivity. The nose must avoid breathing toxic fumes that damage its sense of smell. The mind robbed of the nose's sense of smell is weakened, as it perceives less. The nose that cannot smell fire shall burn.

The nose must smell different scents and odors to smell one smell amongst many and many smells amongst one. It must learn the smell of different herbs and spices, flowers and trees, birds and animals. It must smell ginger to know ginger, a eucalypt to know a eucalypt, and a cow to know a cow.

The nose can perceive over a million different smells, but it can identify only some of them. Conditioning the nose increases its ability to identify more of the smells that it perceives. The more smells the nose learns, the better the nose can identify one smell amongst many and many smells amongst one. Moving through a forest, the conditioned nose smells moisture in the air, rotting leaves on the ground, the bark surrounding trees, and the scent of cologne on the breeze.

The nose must smell different people to identify a person by their scent. Each body smells different, as each body has its own unique scent. This scent is shaped by the body's sex and genetic inheritance. Men smell different from women and family members smell different from strangers.

Each family carries its own scent. The body inherits its scent from its parents just as it inherits the color of its eyes and its hair. It is the first scent a baby's nose learns. It is the scent an adult's nose knows best. By learning its family's scent, the nose also learns to recognize the scent of strangers. The conditioned nose knows when a woman enters a room and if that woman is a sister, a friend, or a stranger, without the eye needing to see her face nor the ear needing to hear her voice.

The stronger the nose's sense of smell grows, the more scents the nose can identify. When the nose can identify men, women, family, and strangers by their scent, then the nose can learn to smell emotions. Each emotion has its own scent. The body releases these scents in response to the emotions that the mind feels. Fear smells different from courage, love smells different from hate. When the mind is calm and the nose is conditioned, then the nose can identify the emotions of others. The mind can keep the eyes steady and stop the muscles from trembling, but it cannot hide the scent of fear.

The body must find a place free of distraction to further condition the nose's sense of smell. It must shut its eyes, close its mouth, and block its ears. The mind can then focus its attention on the smells that surround the body and concentrate on strengthening the nose's ability to identify those smells.

The nose must perform actions such as these until the mind no longer needs to guide the nose toward smells that strengthen it and away from smells that weaken it.

The nose must perform these actions until it guides itself. Once the nose smells what strengthens it and avoids what weakens it without the guidance of the mind and conscious thought, then the nose is disciplined.

The Hand

The hand consists of the fingers, the palm, the elbow, and the arm. God created the hand to evolve. He created the hand to strengthen the body's ability to manipulate its environment, to defend itself, and to express the thoughts of the mind. He created the hand to help the mind to walk the straight path.

The hand must be conditioned to strengthen itself. It is conditioned through the conscious direction of the mind. The mind must direct the hand to perform actions that increase its strength, dexterity, and sensitivity and to avoid actions that weaken it, slow it, and dull its touch. It must guide the hand away from inaction and sloth, which slacken the hand's muscles and deaden its nerves. It must restrain the hand from compulsively caressing objects so the mind focuses on the purpose of the soul rather than on the sensual pleasures of the body. The disciplined hand grasps the straight path. The lazy hand grasps dust.

The hand must exercise and labor regularly to become stronger. It must perform push-ups and climb cliffs. It must carry sacks of grain and lift bricks. These actions strengthen the hand's muscles, nerves, bones, and skin. The stronger the hand becomes, the better it can wield a hammer to build a house, grasp a shovel to dig a garden, and lift a friend who has fallen.

The hand must catch and throw objects to increase its dexterity. It must act together with the eye when catching and throwing balls and sticks to learn how long it takes an object to move from one point to another. It must learn to manipulate itself and gain greater control of its muscles, nerves, and bones. It must move parts of itself alone and in unison. It must touch its ring finger to its thumb, its fingertips to its palm one after another, and flex two phalanges of a finger rather than three. These actions increase the hand's reflexes and speed. The more dexterous the hand becomes, the better it can deflect a blow, grab a rail, and unravel a knot.

The hand must feel the texture of objects to increase its sensitivity. It must feel strands of wool and the grain of wood. It must play instruments such as the piano and the shamisen. It must push and yield against another body to learn the force another body projects so as to know when to resist and when to yield. The more the hand performs these actions, the more sensitive it becomes. The more sensitive the hand becomes, the more the mind perceives and the more easily the mind walks the straight path.

The hand must learn how to defend the body against harm. If the hand cannot defend the body, then the body shall get injured. And if the body is injured, then it is less able to defend itself and defend the straight path. A wish won't hold back a whip. The fate of the Moriori* awaits those who refuse to defend the mind and the body and to resist injustice and lies.

The hand must aim for speed and precision in all its movements. It must remain relaxed beside the body, always ready to respond to whatever the body encounters.

---

* The Moriori were a Polynesian tribe who lived on the Chatham Islands and practised nonviolent resistance to resolve conflict amongst themselves. In the nineteenth century, they were enslaved by Maori from the North Island of New Zealand, despite attempting to nonviolently resist the Maori invasion of their islands.

It must practice striking and grabbing, blocking and deflecting. It must learn the pressure points of the body and how to strike them so as to subdue an attacker quickly.

The hand must learn how to defend the mind. It must learn how to express the thoughts of the mind clearly with the written word so as to defend truth and expose falsehood. It must learn how to remind others of the straight path and further God's will. To express the thoughts of the mind clearly, the hand must write with both pen and keyboard. It must learn how to describe a thing clearly. It must learn how to construct an argument, fashion a thesis, and use evidence to support that thesis. It must learn logic and use logic as a tool to elaborate truth.

Begin conditioning the hand at an early age when the flesh, nerves, muscles, and bones are more malleable and adapt more eagerly to the actions they perform. The hand conditioned from youth strikes faster, harder, and more precisely than the hand that begins conditioning itself in adulthood. This is the same for all the senses and members of the body. The body evolves in response to the actions it performs. The earlier the conditioning of the body begins, the stronger the body becomes.

The flesh of the body slows the thoughts of the mind. This inhibits the mind's ability to meet threats to the body. To overcome this weakness, the body has evolved to react spontaneously to a threat as soon as it arises without the intervention of conscious thought. God has given the body this ability to protect it from harm.

Conditioning increases this ability. The hand must be conditioned to the point at which it reacts spontaneously to a threat without the need for the mind's conscious intervention. The hand conditioned to this point acts more quickly than the hand that needs thought to direct its actions. This is the same for all the senses and members of the body. The conditioned hand catches the falling glass. The unconditioned hand cannot stop the glass from falling.

The hand must perform actions such as these until the mind no longer needs to guide the hand toward what strengthens it and away from what weakens it. The hand must perform these actions until it guides itself.

The hand is disciplined once it effectively manipulates its environment and defends the body and the mind against harm. It is disciplined once it performs actions that strengthen it and avoids actions that weaken it without the guidance of the mind and conscious thought. Only then can the hand help the mind to walk the straight path.

The Foot

The foot consists of the toes, the heel, the leg, and the knee. God created the foot to evolve. He created the foot to aid the movement of the body and to defend the body against harm. He created the foot to help the mind to walk the straight path.

The foot must be conditioned to strengthen itself. It is conditioned through the conscious direction of the mind. The mind conditions the foot by encouraging the foot to perform actions that increase the foot's speed, dexterity, endurance, and ability to defend the body against harm and by restraining the foot from performing actions that weaken the foot. The lazy foot forgets how to run, then walk, and finally crawl. The disciplined foot steps onto the straight path.

The foot must run regularly to increase its speed. It must sprint short distances and jog long distances. It must leap over fences and duck under branches, dodge between pillars and weave between walls. The quicker the foot becomes, the better the body can avoid what should be avoided and meet what must be met.

The foot must aim for grace and balance in all its movements to increase its dexterity. It must maintain a light and fluid motion so that the energy the body expends on moving is used efficiently and so that the body can respond to unforeseen circumstances as they arise. It must avoid plodding and erratic movements that waste the body's energy and reduce the body's capacity to avoid obstacles.

The foot must raise its awareness of itself and its surroundings to increase its dexterity. It must be aware of what lies ahead of it and what lies behind it. It must know where its next step shall land before it places it. It must be constantly aware. In this way, the foot shall avoid holes and remain on solid ground.

The foot must climb and jump to increase its dexterity. It must climb up trees and scramble down girders, scale up cliff faces and negotiate ridges. It must jump over pits and bound between buildings, leap off roofs and spring up to ledges. It should find a shoot of bamboo and jump over it each day. As the shoot of bamboo grows higher, so shall the foot learn to jump higher.

The foot must walk to increase its endurance. It must walk each day rather than drive or catch a bus or train. It must hike in rugged regions, through forests and along mountain ranges to learn how to walk long distances and to follow winding and undulating paths. It must make pilgrimage to the holy places where the prophets have spread the message of God. This increases the endurance of the foot and encourages the mind to forget the distractions of the body and focus instead upon the purpose of the soul.

The foot must learn how to defend the body against harm. It must learn how to kick with speed and accuracy and block an attacker's blows. It must learn how to target the pressure points and vulnerable areas of the body so as to subdue an attacker quickly. It must kick a punching bag or spar with a partner to increase its speed and accuracy, and to learn to gauge distance correctly. Once it understands the distance between itself and another, it can intercept and deflect blows away from the body. The foot must also develop flexibility to fully utilize the force created by itself and the torso. It must perform stretching exercises to achieve this. He who cannot defend himself cannot defend the straight path.

The foot must be conditioned to react spontaneously to a threat as soon as it arises without the need of conscious thought. The foot that reacts spontaneously moves more quickly than the foot that requires thought to direct its actions. The foot gains this ability through constant and regular practice.

Begin conditioning the foot at an early age when its flesh, nerves, muscles, and bones are still growing and are more able to adapt to strenuous action. The foot conditioned from youth is better able to meet the demands placed upon it in adulthood. It is better able to trek long distances and climb high mountains. It is better able to struggle and overcome hardship.

When conditioning the foot, avoid repetitive exercises that desensitize nerves, strain muscles, and fracture bones. The nerves, muscles, and bones work in unison rather than in isolation. If only one part of the foot is strengthened, then it becomes unbalanced and injury occurs. Perform actions that strengthen the different parts of the foot at the same time rather than only one part, as this is the best way to avoid injury. This is the same for the other senses and members of the body.

The foot must perform actions such as these until the mind no longer needs to guide the foot toward what strengthens it and away from what weakens it. The foot must perform these actions until it guides itself.

The foot is disciplined once it walks farther, runs more quickly, dodges faster, jumps longer, climbs higher, and defends the body against harm. It is disciplined once it performs actions that strengthen it and avoids actions that weaken it without the guidance of the mind and conscious thought. Only then can the foot help the mind to walk the straight path.

The Torso

God created the torso to evolve. He created the torso as the pillar of the body to support the head, the arms, and the legs and to house and protect the heart, the lungs, the liver, and the other vital organs. He created the torso to store the body's energy, focus it, and release it.

The torso must be conditioned to strengthen it. It is conditioned through the conscious direction of the mind. The mind conditions the torso by encouraging the torso to perform actions that increase the torso's flexibility, strength, and endurance and augment the movements of the hands and the feet, and by avoiding actions that weaken the torso. A conditioned torso is the foundation of a disciplined body. Blessed is the conditioned torso. It shall help the hand to grip longer and the foot to walk farther. Pity the lazy torso. It shall deny the hand's grasp and the foot's step.

The torso must perform actions that loosen and strengthen the muscles of the spine and abdomen to increase its flexibility and strength. It must walk, run, and swim and perform regular exercises such as sit-ups and push-ups. It must perform yoga to enable the back to bend farther. This exercise opens the lungs, enabling them to draw more air with each breath, increasing the oxygen in the blood and the body's energy. It also increases the circulation of the blood through the body, helping the body to digest food and liquid more quickly, process nutrients more efficiently, and further increase its energy.

The spine of the torso must remain straight and relaxed, neither stooped nor rigid. The stooped torso is a sign of a mind lacking dignity. It compels the eyes to stare down at the ground, blinding the eyes to what lies ahead. The rigid torso wastes the body's energy in retaining its rigidity. A straight and relaxed torso is a sign of a healthy and dignified mind and body.

The torso must seek harsh environments to increase its endurance. It must seek deserts and snow plains, mountain paths and dense forests. When the torso lives in a desert, it is forced to learn to expend heat more quickly to reduce its own temperature so as not to overheat. When the torso lives in the snow, it is forced to learn to conserve its own heat more efficiently so as not to freeze. Extreme environments strengthen the torso and condition the body to endure hardship more easily. The body adapts to its environment.

The torso stores and focuses the body's energy. The hand and the foot draw on the body's energy when they move. The more relaxed the hand and the foot, the more easily the body's energy flows through their nerves, muscles, and bones and the faster and stronger are their movements. The relaxed hand that moves in unison with the torso, and tightens its muscles at the moment of impact, strikes harder and faster than the rigid hand that moves separately from the torso.

The torso decays in old age: nerves become numb, muscles slacken, and bones grow brittle. Yet old age is no excuse for inaction nor for the torso to stop conditioning itself, for the torso remains an instrument of God's will until its last breath and can only achieve God's will by retaining its strength.

Conditioning enables the torso to retain its strength. It slows the effects of aging and holds decay at bay. The elderly woman who conditions her torso and legs can walk five kilometers before tiring, whereas the elderly woman who is lazy can barely lift herself off the couch. The torso must continue to condition itself throughout its life so as to achieve its purpose. This is the same for all the senses and members of the body.

The torso must perform actions such as these until the mind no longer needs to guide the torso toward what strengthens it and away from what weakens it. The torso must perform these actions until it guides itself.

The torso is disciplined once it is flexible, strong, and can endure hardship. It is disciplined once it performs actions that strengthen it and avoids actions that weaken it without the guidance of the mind and conscious thought. Only then can the torso help the mind to walk the straight path.

V. Religion

God gave religion to humanity so the soul, the mind, and the body need not walk the straight path alone.

An individual can achieve much. He can set an example for others to emulate and so strengthen themselves. However, a group is far stronger than an individual and can achieve far more because a group combines the efforts of many. Jesus Christ, Mahatma Gandhi, and Dr. Martin Luther King Jr. did not act alone. Each of them was a member of a group. Each of them achieved justice and strengthened humanity with the help of others. God wants us to help each other so that we grow stronger together.

God fashions each of us as an extension of humanity. We are conceived by a mother and a father and are born into a family and a society. We benefit from the ideas and achievements of others and depend upon what others have made to survive; our every creation a product of their creations. Only the fool believes he is solely responsible for his achievements. A person invented the computer you type on, another made the car you drive, and another wove the clothes you wear. A thousand hands invented the pen. God created us to struggle together to evolve and fulfil His will.

Yet just as there is no guarantee that a seed shall grow into a tree, so too is our own evolution not guaranteed. All that we have achieved could be lost. We could lose everything through arrogance, laziness, greed, and fear. Vice rots all things. It weakens the mind and the body, and it retards evolution.

No longer can we stumble forward, heedless of the effects of our actions upon our minds and bodies and upon the minds and the bodies of our children. We must begin to guide our own evolution. We must seek virtue and reject vice, for only virtue strengthens the mind and the body. Only virtue guarantees the evolution of humanity.

Humanity needs a plan to guide its evolution. It needs an evolutionary plan that spans generations. This evolutionary plan must encourage and support the virtuous acts of individuals and emphasize the necessity of mental and physical conditioning for disciplining and strengthening the mind and the body. It must teach that only by walking the straight path is humanity's evolution guaranteed.

An individual, alone, cannot implement this evolutionary plan, because the life of an individual is too brief. Only a group can do this. Only a group can follow a consistent course of action from one generation to the next to achieve a purpose. Only a group can implement a plan that takes centuries to fulfil.

The group most capable of implementing this evolutionary plan is a religion. Religions survive longer than any other groups. As corporations, nations, and empires rise and fall, religions remain. Only religions have the strength of purpose needed to implement a plan that spans generations, because only religions seek virtue and reject vice and are dedicated to walking the straight path.

Soon a religion shall form to guide humanity's evolution. This is inevitable, for humanity shall see the necessity for such a religion and create it. The religion shall spread the message that only by walking the straight path is the evolution of humanity guaranteed. The religion's voice shall be soft in the beginning, but it shall grow louder as the religion performs virtuous acts and gains new members. And as its voice grows louder, more people shall hear the religion's message and begin to walk the straight path.

The religion shall face many challenges. But it shall achieve its purpose only if its members are well organized and highly disciplined. They must be united, and they can be united only when they are loyal to one another.

The basis of loyalty is equality and respect. All members of the religion must share equally in its duties, achievements, and setbacks. They must struggle together and face the same hardships. If one member eats only rice, then all members must eat only rice. If one member cleans a toilet, then all members must clean a toilet. Only if the leaders of the religion suffer the same hardships as the members of the religion shall the leaders understand what the members suffer and lead the religion wisely.

The leaders of the religion must avoid granting themselves privileges. Privileges are inequitable and unjust. They divide people. They shall divide the leaders from the members of the religion. They shall make the members disloyal to one another and undermine the members' organization and discipline.

Once divided, a religion decays and is unable to rectify injustice and fulfil the will of God. It steps from the straight path. Pity the divided religion. It is dust in the wind.

A religion is its members, not its possessions. Food, buildings, wealth, and land can be replaced but people cannot. So the leaders of the religion must look to the welfare of its members first and other things second. This shall make the members loyal to one another and create a bond of trust between them and the religion. This bond shall become a reservoir of immense strength for the reli gion during times of adversity.

The religion must have an effective leadership. It must be able to identify and appoint capable leaders. A capable leader is intelligent and wise. He acts virtuously and avoids vice. He leads from the front and shares the hardships of those he leads. He treats others with respect and dignity and gives them the opportunity to strengthen themselves. He also places the needs of the religion before the needs of himself. A capable leader walks the straight path.

By acting virtuously, a leader inspires others to act virtuously. By leading from the front, he can use his initiative to respond to unforeseen circumstances as they arise, allowing the religion to avoid mistakes, take advantage of opportunities, and achieve its purpose. By leading from the front, he also shares the hardships of those he leads and inspires them to struggle harder and make greater sacrifices to achieve the religion's purpose.

Shared struggle unifies a religion. It strengthens all its members and encourages them to act virtuously. Powerful indeed is a religion whose members act together, for one another, so that they can strengthen humanity and fulfil the will of God. God guides such religions and those who walk the straight path.

The leaders of the religion must be wary of arrogance and never place their own goals before those of the religion. They should never mistake the religion for God nor place the religion above God. God loves one religion no more than another, as a mother loves one of her children no more than another. God loves all religions equally because all religions seek the straight path and are instruments of His will. The arrogant are blind to this. They reject God when they place religion above God. And so the arrogant fall.

The universe is full of distraction. Those who no longer hear their souls easily lose their way. Even the strongest can falter when all around them say that right is wrong and wrong is right. The religion shall provide a refuge for the righteous and a beacon for those who have stumbled in the dark. It shall speak a message of truth and freedom and spread the words of the prophets to those who need them most.

God demands that we evolve. He demands that we strengthen ourselves so that we learn more about the universe, walk the straight path, and draw closer to Him. The religion shall fall if it forgets this and cares only for its wealth and power. It shall wither like the unwatered fruit. But if the religion acts virtuously and fulfils the will of God, then it shall outlast nations and empires. Nothing can stand in the way of such an instrument, an instrument fashioned to strengthen humanity.

About the Author

Christian Edward is a teacher and an author. He lives in Melbourne, Australia, and holds a Bachelor of Arts Degree, a Graduate Diploma in Education, a Post-Graduate Diploma in History, and a Master of Arts Degree in Renaissance History and Philosophy. He currently teaches the Russian and Chinese Revolutions, and Asian History to high school students. He has presented at educational conferences on teaching Asian History, and has written several chapters on Ancient Chinese and Medieval Japanese History in a number of educational textbooks.

www.ingramcontent.com/pod-product-compliance
Lightning Source LLC
LaVergne TN
LVHW091226080426
835509LV00009B/1189